994
SAU

HERON ISLAND

on Australia's Great Barrier Reef

Dave Saunders

Dryad Press Limited   London

The Islands series

What have these people in common: Enid Blyton, Daniel Defoe, Robert Louis Stevenson and Roy Plomley? They have all written about islands, islands as places of adventure or fantasy. Think for a moment of the many stories or events that are associated with islands. What do you know about "Fortress Falklands", or Alcatraz, or the adventures of Robinson Crusoe? Islands have long held a special appeal and this series sets out to explore the fascination of islands.

Every island is unique, with a different location, a distinctive history and a particular personality. And yet about them all there are similarities, too. Island cultures are distinct because they are isolated, set apart from mainstream societies. They are remote, places of refuge or sanctuary, where you can "get away from it all"! Monks and rich recluses have chosen island homes because they wanted seclusion. Other island inhabitants have had no choice in the matter because the isolation of islands also makes them ideal places for imprisonment or exile; Alcatraz and Elba certainly have that one thing in common.

In many cases, too, the remoteness of islands has meant that life for people, animals and plants has remained undisturbed by the progress and change of the mainlands. Forms and ways of life survive which elsewhere have become extinct, as is the case on the remote and beautiful islands of the Galapagos.

Another common feature of island life is that it can present similar problems of survival. Is there enough land to grow food and to keep animals? Is there an ample supply of water? Why do islands become deserted?

Islands, therefore, can be places of challenge where you must learn to survive, fending for yourself on limited resources, or places of isolation and retreat where you dream about the good life — and listen to your desert island discs!

In each book of the series the author's purpose is to explore the uniqueness of a particular island and to convey the special appeal of the island. There is no common approach but in every case the island can be seen as a system in which a society is linked to its physical environment. An island culture can show clearly how the natural environment influences the ways people make a living. It also shows how people learn to modify or change that environment to make life better or more secure. This is very much a geographical view of islands, but the ideas and study skills used in the books are not limited to those of the geographer. The one controlling idea of the series is that islands are special places; small enough to know well and varied enough to illustrate the rich diversity of environments and lifestyles from all parts of the world. Islands can be places of social experiment or strategic importance, of simple survival or extravagance. Islands are the world in miniature.

John Bentley
Series editor

For details of other books in the Islands series, please write to Dryad Press Limited, 8 Cavendish Square, London W1M 0AJ.

Contents

	Island information	4
	Introduction	5
1	Finding it	6
2	A cay is born	10
3	The first resort	15
4	What makes the island tick?	19
5	The daily round	24
6	Life on land	31
7	The green turtle	37
8	Reef life	44
9	Taking the plunge	48
10	Interests of science	56
	PS Blueprint for survival	60
	Glossary	62
	Further reading	63
	Index	64

ACKNOWLEDGMENTS

My special thanks go to Sheila Saunders, Reg O'Grady, the Queensland Travel & Tourist Corporation, the Australian Tourist Commission, Qantas Airways, Queensland National Parks & Wildlife Service, Great Barrier Reef Marine Park Authority, University of Queensland Heron Island Research Station, P & O Air Holidays and Heron Island Pty Ltd.

All photographs and diagrams, on the cover and inside the book, except for the frontispiece (Queensland National Parks and Wildlife Service), and figures 31 (Heron Island Pty Ltd) and 53 (P&O), are copyright of the author.

All rights reserved. No part of this publication may be reproduced, in any form or by any means, without permission from the publishers.

© Dave Saunders 1987
First published 1987

Typeset by Tek-Art Ltd, Kent
and printed in Great Britain by
R.J. Acford Ltd,
Chichester, Sussex
for the publishers Dryad Press Limited,
8 Cavendish Square, London W1M 0AJ

ISBN 0 8521 9688 1

Island Information

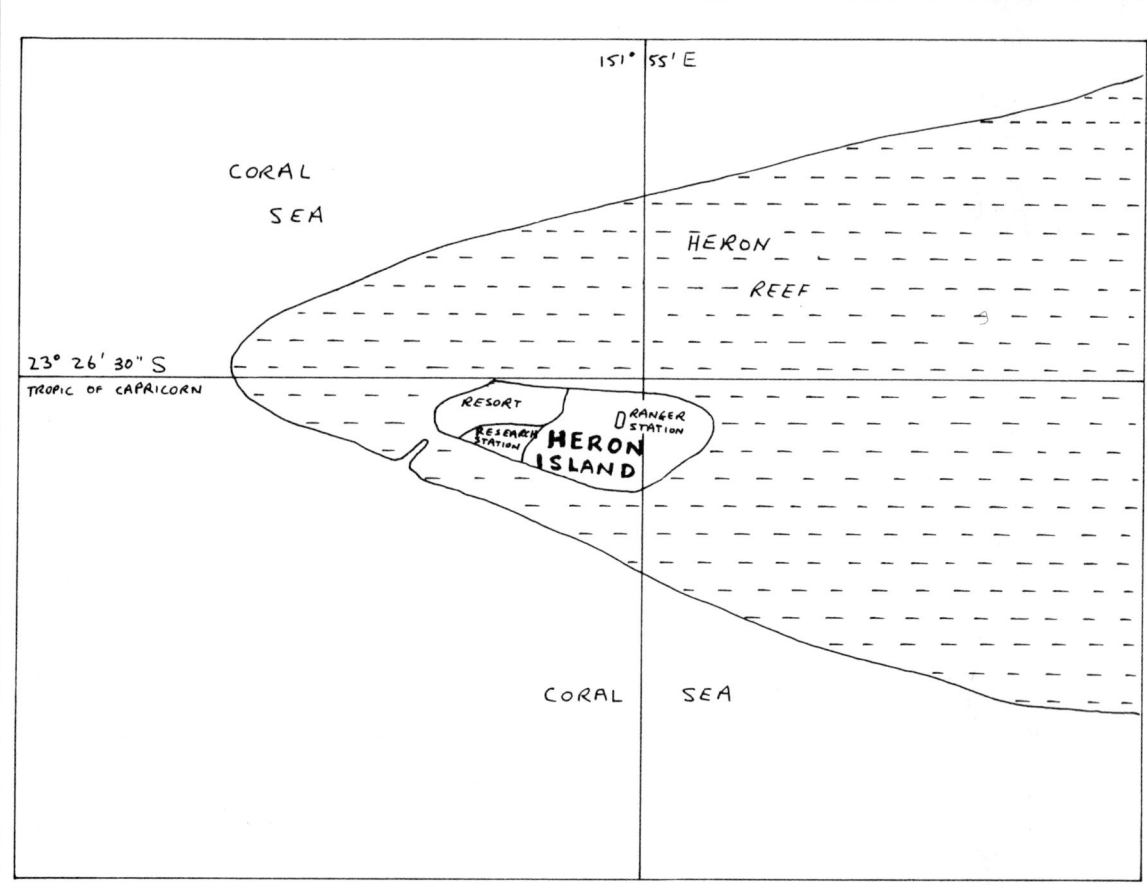

Area: 0.17 sq. km. or 17 hectares or 42 acres

Population: varies between 200 and 300

Population density: 5–7 people per acre

Government: A part of Australia. Affairs of the island are decided by an Island Council made up of representatives from the resort and from the research station and park rangers

Language: English

Currency: Australian dollars.

History:
- 1843 Heron Island was first recorded
- 1923 First settlement – turtle soup factory
- 1947 First regular flights to the island
- 1951 Research station established on the island by the Great Barrier Reef Committee
- 1982 Queensland National Parks and Wildlife Service set up a ranger station on the island

Economy: Tourism

Festivals: Bird Week and Reef Week organized and run by the Queensland National Parks and Wildlife Service and Heron Island Pty Ltd

Introduction

1 *Heron Island from the air.*

What do you think of when you look at this picture? Do you imagine lazy holidays at the beach? A desert island adventure? Or something else?

This is Heron Island. It's a special place. Only a handful of people live here permanently, yet there are usually over two hundred visitors staying on the island. It is very small, yet it never seems crowded. There are no cars nor televisions, yet there is always something interesting going on, as long as you know where to look.

Heron Island is more than just a tropical island; it is a community of people, birds, plants and marine organisms living together in a delicate balance. It is a community that can teach us much about our own values and how we view the world in which we live.

1
Finding it

2 Hardy Reef.

Imagine trying to navigate a ship through this lacework of coral reefs. If you were Captain James Cook or one of the early explorers who braved the southern seas, you would probably have dreaded the Great Barrier Reef. It looks harmless enough, but it is a huge maze of islands and coral reefs which lie mostly beneath the surface of the ocean. In the eighteenth and nineteenth centuries the Reef presented a dangerous hazard to mariners trying to pick a route through the uncharted waters.

The entire region of the Reef stretches for about 1,200 miles, from Lady Elliott Island in the south to Anchor Island near Papua New Guinea. Approximately 1,000 islands and over 2,500 separate reefs are dotted over an area of some 100,000 square miles. In an atlas, turn to a map of the Pacific Ocean. Find the east coast of Australia. Then name three countries situated to the east of it.

Heron Island is situated near the southern end of the Great Barrier Reef, off the north-east coast of Queensland, Australia. You can locate the island by using lines of latitude and longitude.

Latitude and longitude

Lines, or *parallels*, of latitude go around the globe, between the equator and the poles. The equator is the longest line of latitude and is given the value 0°. All other lines of latitude are either north or south of the equator. The North Pole is 90°N and the South Pole is 90°S.

Lines of longitude join the North and South Poles and are all the same length. They are

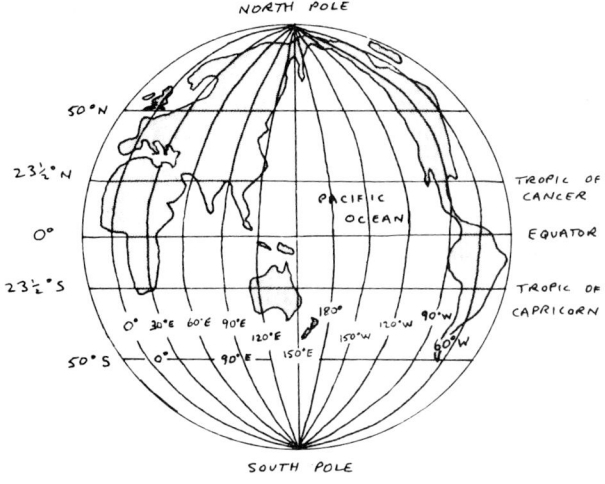

3 A sketch map of the globe, showing lines of latitude and longitude.

The exact position of Heron Island is longitude 151° 55' east, latitude 23° 26' 40" south. Can you locate it on figure 3?

First find the Tropic of Capricorn. This is the line of latitude which circles the southern hemisphere of the globe at 23° 26' 30" south of the equator. The Tropic of Cancer is the line of latitude which lies 23° 26' 30" to the north of the equator. You can remember which is which by thinking of corns on the feet!

On a map of the world find Australia and see where the Tropic of Capricorn crosses the east coast. Heron Island is 45 miles offshore and just south of the Tropic of Capricorn.

Marine park

The cluster of islands and reefs around this area is called the Capricorn Group, which lies in the Capricornia Section of the Great Barrier Reef.

measured from Greenwich in London which is 0°. Lines of longitude are either east or west of the Greenwich line.

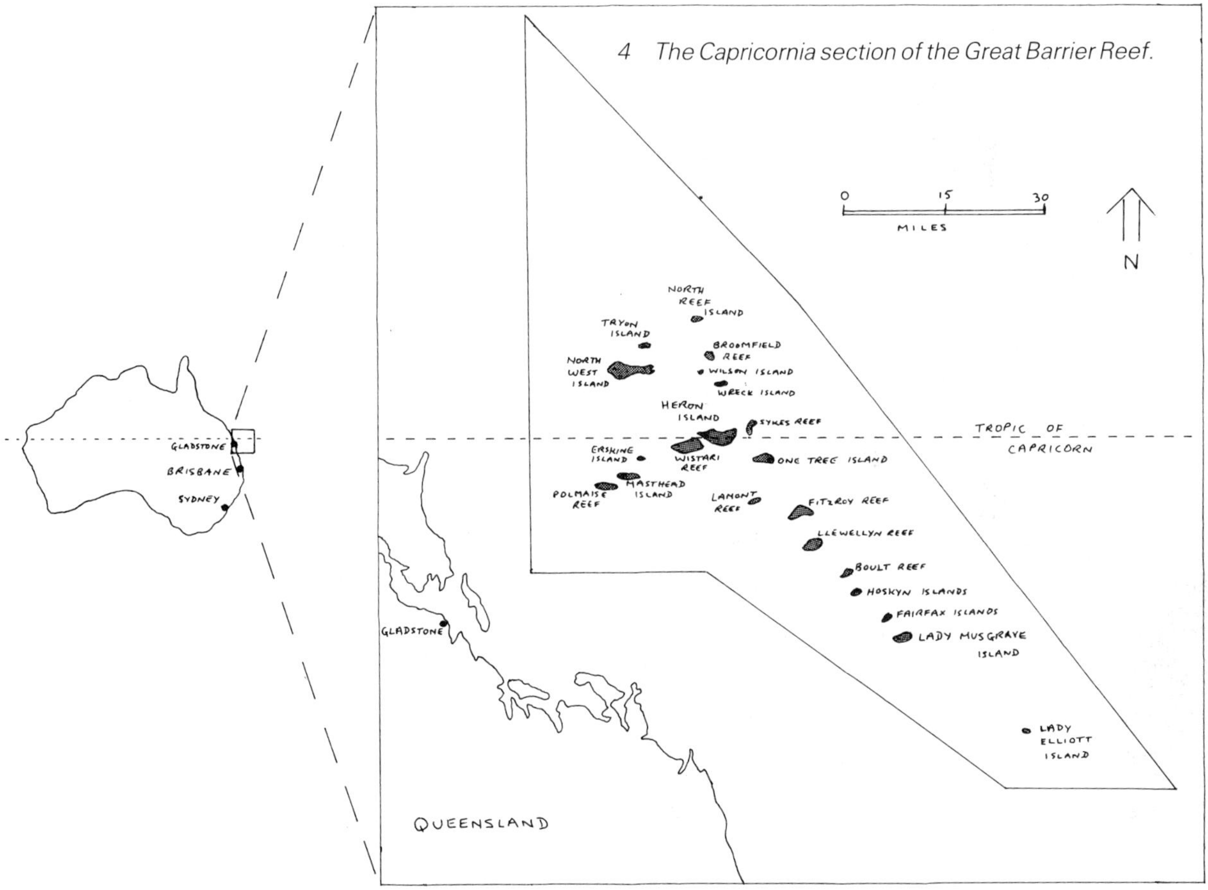

4 The Capricornia section of the Great Barrier Reef.

To protect the natural environment from pollution and over-fishing, Heron and Wistari Reefs were declared a marine park in 1974. Then in 1979 the entire Capricornia Section was proclaimed as the first section of the Great Barrier Reef Marine Park. The park covers about 4,600 square miles and encompasses 34 reefs. Thirteen of these reefs support coral islands, or cays, and one of these is Heron Island.

Can you think why the coral reef does not extend further south than Lady Elliott Island? How far is it from Gladstone to Heron Island? What are some of the ways in which the journey could be made?

The climate

In the southern hemisphere the seasons are the reverse of those in the northern hemisphere. When it is winter in Europe, Asia or North America it is summer in Australia, and vice versa. Christmas is the hottest time of the year on the Great Barrier Reef. On 22nd December (mid-summer) the sun is directly overhead at noon on the Tropic of Capricorn.

On Heron Island the temperature never falls anywhere near freezing point and it is easy to imagine it is summer all year round.

The climate graphs show the rainfall figures for Heron Island and for Sydney (Australia), London (England) and New York (USA). Copy these graphs carefully. Then, using the temperature figures in the table, mark with a dot the average temperature for each month and join the dots together to make a line graph.

5 Climate graphs

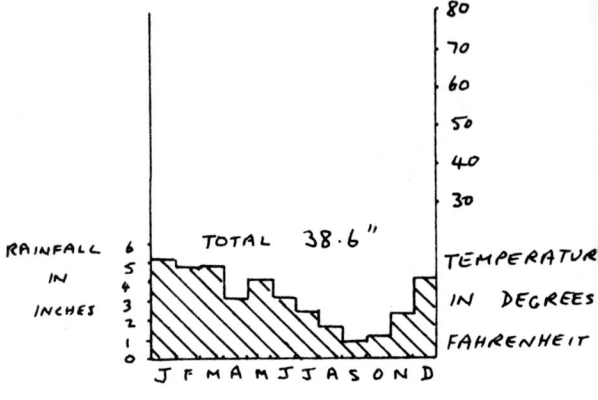

(a) Heron Island

(b) Sydney

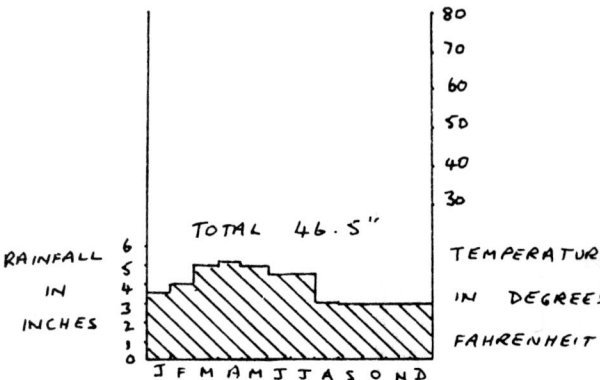

Which place has the highest monthly average temperature? What is the average temperature on Heron Island in July? And in

Monthly average temperatures in degrees Fahrenheit

	Jan.	Feb.	Mar.	Apr.	May	June	July	Aug.	Sept.	Oct.	Nov.	Dec.
Heron Is.	77.0	77.0	73.4	71.6	66.2	60.8	62.6	66.2	66.2	69.8	75.2	77.0
Sydney	71.5	71.5	69.5	64.5	59.0	54.5	53.0	55.5	59.0	63.5	67.0	70.0
London	39.5	40.0	44.0	48.0	54.0	60.0	64.0	63.0	59.0	51.0	44.0	40.5
New York	30.5	31.0	37.5	49.5	60.5	68.5	74.0	73.0	69.5	59.0	44.0	35.0

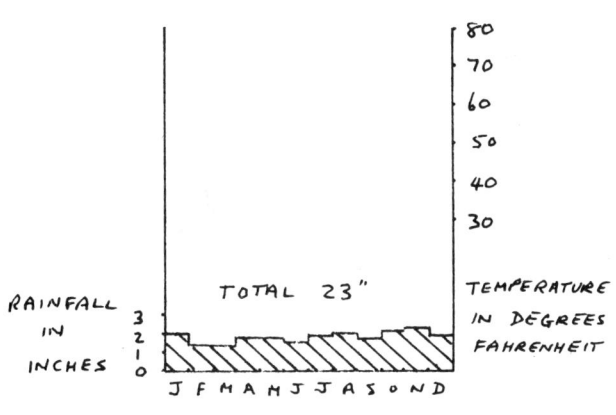

(c) London

(d) New York

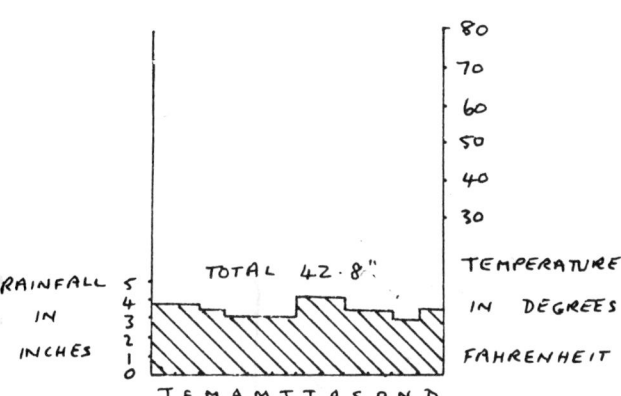

January? Which is Heron Island's driest month? How much rainfall does Heron receive in its wettest month?

Heron receives most of its rainfall during January, February and March. This is the cyclone or monsoon season. Winds laden with moisture after their long journey across the Pacific Ocean occasionally strike the northern part of the Great Barrier Reef with sudden heavy rains. It is rare for the full impact of one of these violent tropical storms to be felt as far south as Heron Island, but the skies are often more overcast and winds are stronger at this time of year.

The climate plays an important role in the life of Heron Island. If the water temperature were much cooler the coral would not be able to survive and the island would never have formed. Turtles are attracted to the island's beaches which are warm enough for hatching their eggs. Birds such as the noddy tern and reef heron like the weather here throughout the year, while migratory birds come to escape the winter in cooler climates.

Thousands of people also visit Heron Island. They come to see the coral reef, the turtles and the birds, as well as to enjoy the sun and the beaches. Before they get to know the island, few realize that it was actually built by animals — countless tiny marine animals.

2
A cay is born

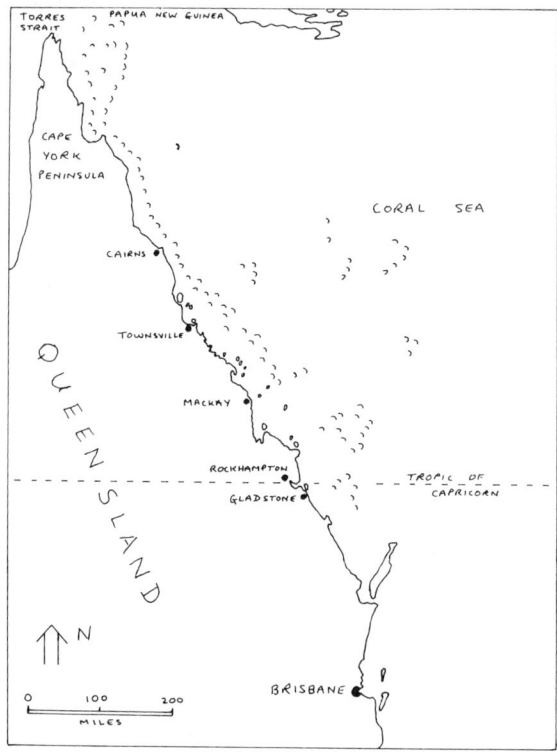

6 North-east Australia and the Great Barrier Reef.

Beneath the surface of the ocean off the coast of eastern Australia is a broad platform or continental shelf. This is a wide ledge where the water is shallow compared to the deep ocean – generally less than 100 fathoms deep (183m). The tropical seas off north-east Queensland are rich in plankton and ideal for the growth of coral reefs.

This was not always the case. Many of the earth's land masses are moving slowly. Some 30 million years ago this region was further south than it is now, and too cold for coral growth. Slowly the continent moved northwards into the tropics, and conditions became suited to the formation of coral. The northern, warmer section began its life 25 million years ago, but the foundations of most of the Great Barrier Reef are just 2 million years old. The coral reefs we can see today began after the last ice age and represent only 8-10,000 years of growth by generations of tiny coral polyps.

Coral polyps look like plants but in fact are living animals with soft bodies. These primitive creatures take calcium and lime from the water and build themselves protective limestone cups. They are similar to small sea anemones, and come in many colours, from yellow to purple.

The coral reef has many surprises. The different species of polyp form different shapes and grow at different rates. Branching staghorn coral grows about 25cm a year, whereas brain coral increases by only 1cm or 2cm a year.

Not all corals are brightly coloured. Most are a shade of brown. If you go deeper than about 10m, even the brilliant red and orange corals appear black or grey. This is because water is less transparent than air and so does not let as much light pass through it. The deeper you go the darker it becomes, because the sea absorbs the light of the sun's rays. The different colours of the spectrum are absorbed, one at a time. Red disappears at about 5m below the surface, then orange at about 10m. Yellow is absorbed at about 15m, green at

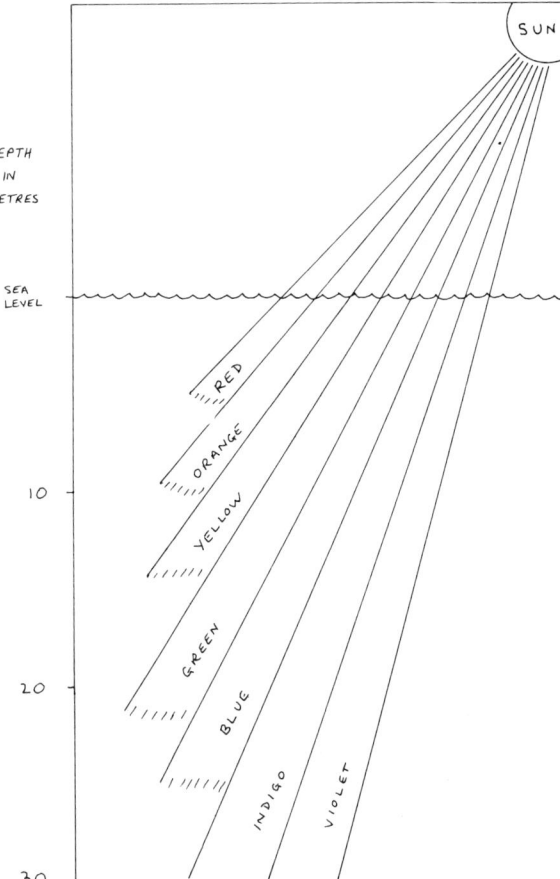

more slowly than coral in the warmer waters of the northern Great Barrier Reef, and reef-forming corals cannot grow at all further south than Lady Elliott Island.

The reef-building corals are part of a class of corals called Anthozoa. When the polyps die, they leave their limestone skeletons and the next generation of polyps builds on top of this, forming a coral colony.

Coral colonies increase in size when a new polyp "buds" off the polyp next to it. The strange and varied shapes of coral colonies are partly the result of more rapid budding in particular directions.

Corals also reproduce sexually by releasing small, swimming larvae, or planulae, which may settle and begin a new colony.

Corals need sunlight. Colonies continually grow up towards the surface and cannot exist deeper than 30 fathoms (about 55m). They thrive in clear, unpolluted salt water which is free from sediment.

During the day the polyp retracts into its tubular skeleton. But at feeding time, usually at

7 Colour absorption. White sunlight is made up of several different colours – red, orange, yellow, green, blue, indigo, violet – the colours of the spectrum. As the sun's rays pass through water, the colours are absorbed one at a time, starting with the red end of the spectrum. Below about 30m everything appears to be grey or black.

8 Coral polyp feeding. It is approximately 15mm high and 2-3mm across.

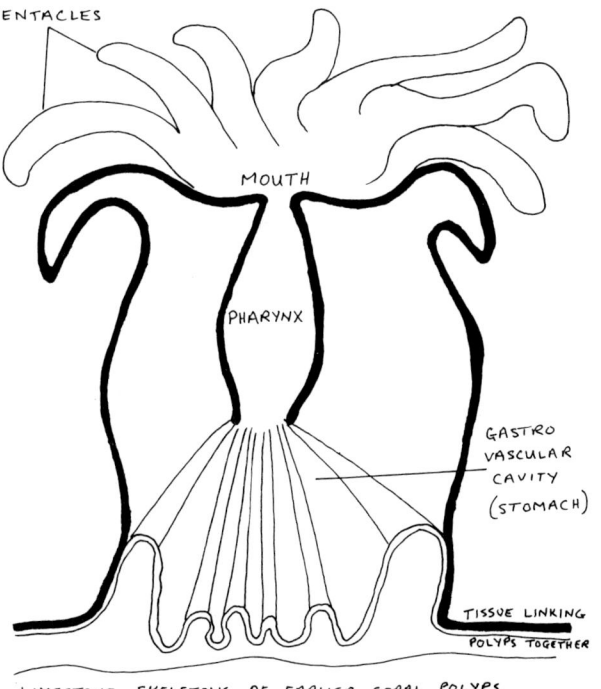

about 22m and blue at about 26m. When a colour is absorbed objects of that colour appear to be black, so, at 10m, red and orange corals look black, yet you can still distinguish yellows, greens and blues. If you shine a torch beam or flashlight from an underwater camera onto the coral, the natural colours will be revealed.

Building a reef

Polyps cannot live if the temperature of the sea water falls below about 18°C (64.4°F). This usually restricts them to the tropical or subtropical region between latitudes 30° north and 30° south. The coral of Heron Island grows

night, the polyp emerges from its cup and stretches out its poisonous tentacles. These tentacles eject potent "harpoons" into the plankton which is then digested in the polyp's stomach. Most coral is harmless to humans, though the brown and yellow fire coral can sting or burn if touched by bare skin.

Algae lend a hand

Tiny plant cells called zooxanthellae (algae) live within the coral tissue. The algae converts sunlight into oxygen and food for the polyps. The mutually beneficial relationship between the algae and the polyps is an example of symbiosis. The algae enjoy the protection given by the coral skeleton and also use the waste products discarded by the polyp. This removal of waste helps the polyp grow more efficiently. Such a symbiotic relationship occurs in hard and soft corals, clams and many other marine organisms.

The construction of the reef is aided by the addition of the remains of starfish, sea urchins and sea cucumbers, while certain limestone-producing algae help to cement the spaces between the dead coral.

Coral cannot live for long out of the water, though tougher corals can survive being exposed to the air for several hours. The low-tide level usually marks the end of coral growth and this often creates flat-topped coral colonies.

Sometimes waves pile up pieces of broken coral above the level of high tide. As more debris and sand accumulate a tiny island, or islet, is born, perched on top of a much larger coral platform.

In this way, thousands of years and numerous generations of polyps have produced the Great Barrier Reef. It is the largest structure on the face of the earth created by living organisms. Heron Island is just one of the many thin caps of sand on top of the compacted skeletons or dead polyps estimated to be 150m thick.

◀ 9 A variety of plants have successfully established themselves in the limestone soil which is formed from broken-down coral. The plants help to hold the sand particles together and they provide shelter and nesting sites for sea birds.

How plants arrive

Once the island is formed other processes begin to take place. Vegetation is introduced and becomes established on the newly formed islet. Among the first plants to take hold are creepers or convolvuli, which help to bind the sand particles together and prevent them being washed away again by the next storm.

Plant seeds can arrive on the island in several ways. You could draw a sketch or diagram to illustrate the methods by which the various plants first came to Heron Island:

- Creepers have buoyant seeds which can withstand sea water. They float on the surface and are washed ashore, establishing themselves on the beach.
- The seeds of she-oaks are very light and have wings which enable them to be carried by the wind. Although many are lost at sea, a few settle on the island.
- Birds may land on this mini-island and leave guano containing seeds of shrubs and trees.
- The sticky fruit of the pisonia tree sticks to the feathers and legs of sea birds and is sometimes brushed off when they stop to rest on the island.

"Low" and "high" islands

Heron is a true coral island or "cay", a word taken from the Spanish *cayo*, meaning islet. Cay is usually pronounced "key", the same as the "Keys" on the Florida coast of America.

True coral cays, called the "low islands", originated as coral growths from the sea bed.

Other islands ("high islands") off the Queensland coast are continental islands of granite and other igneous rock. They were once part of the mainland which was drowned when the land subsided and the coastal region was flooded.

The "high islands" sometimes reach heights of over 1,100m. They are often clothed in dense jungle and have a greater variety of plants than Heron Island. Although these islands are not made of coral, many have fringing reefs.

Heron is the highest island in the Capricorn Group, yet it rises to only about 5m above sea level. The cay is just 200m wide (north-south)

10 Some of the Whitsunday group of islands. ▶ These are "high islands".

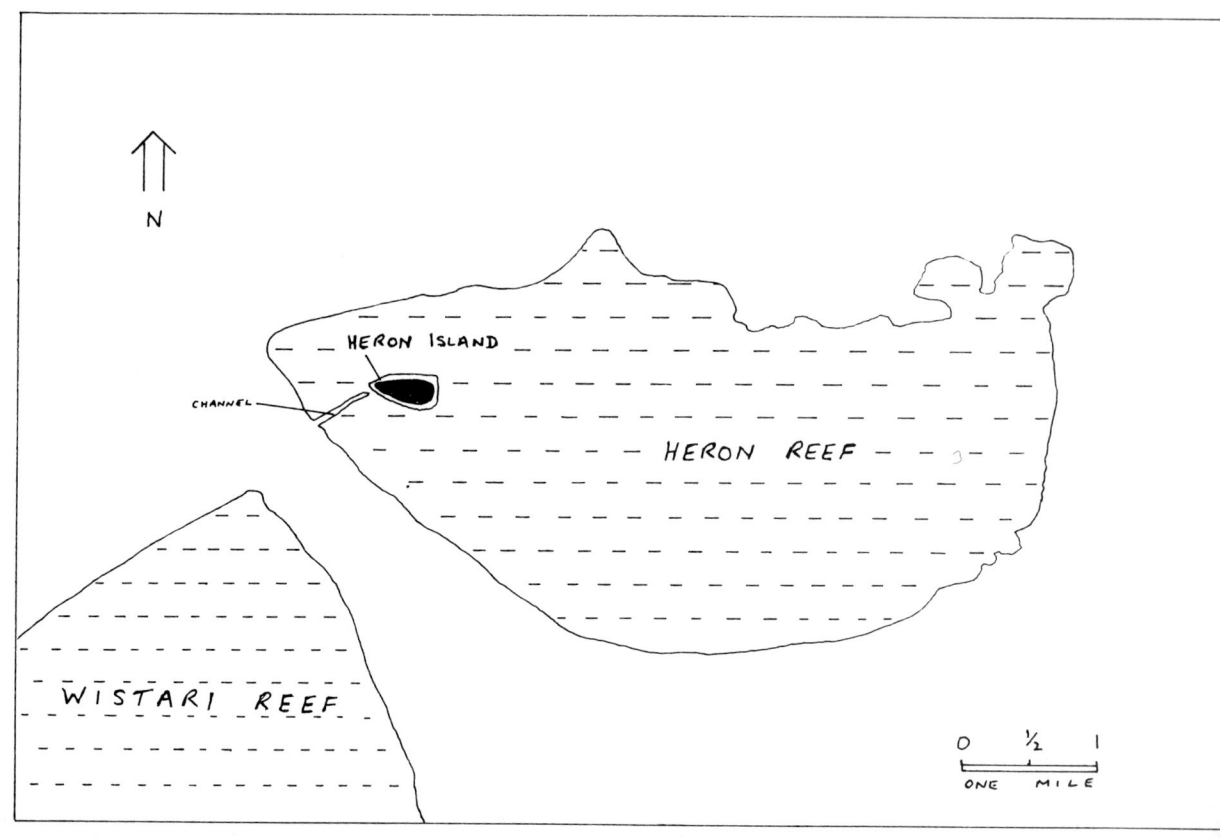

and half a mile long (west-east). It covers 42 acres — about the size of 23 football pitches. You could walk right around it in forty minutes, though most people prefer to take a lot longer.

11 *Heron Island, Heron Reef and Wistari Reef.*

Perched on a platform

Heron Island is situated at the western end of a broad coral platform — Heron Reef. On one side it is nearly half a mile from the island to deep water, while to the east the platform extends for about five miles. The platform or reef that supports the cay covers some 12 square miles and is enormous compared with the small, wooded sand hill.

The oval shape of the island is determined largely by the strength and duration of the prevailing winds. The limy sand on the weathered side of the island, the side facing south and south-east, has been consolidated into beach rock. This slows down the rate at which the island is eroded by the wind and waves.

This idyllic cay surrounded by white sandy beaches and beautiful coral formations may seem the obvious place for a holiday resort, yet the first human inhabitants of Heron Island had something very different in mind.

3

The first resort

On 12th January 1843 a British Royal Navy corvette, the HMS *Fly*, was surveying the southern end of the Great Barrier Reef. It anchored off a tiny coral cay covered with a dense growth of pisonia trees.

The geologist on board, Joseph Beete Jukes, viewed the island from the ship's masthead, then described it in his journal: "A small island, with a white sand beach and a tuft of trees, is surrounded by a symmetrically oval space of water of the bright grass-green colour, enclosed by a ring of glittering surf, as white as snow, immediately outside of which is the rich dark blue of deep water."

Noticing the large numbers of herons, he named the coral cay Heron Island.

Before buildings began to be erected on Heron Island it looked much like the island in the photograph below. Imagine you have been asked to survey the island with a view to establishing a settlement there. How would you describe it in your report? Make a list of the things you would need to support a small community of people on the island.

12 Wilson Island, an uninhabited island of the Great Barrier Reef.

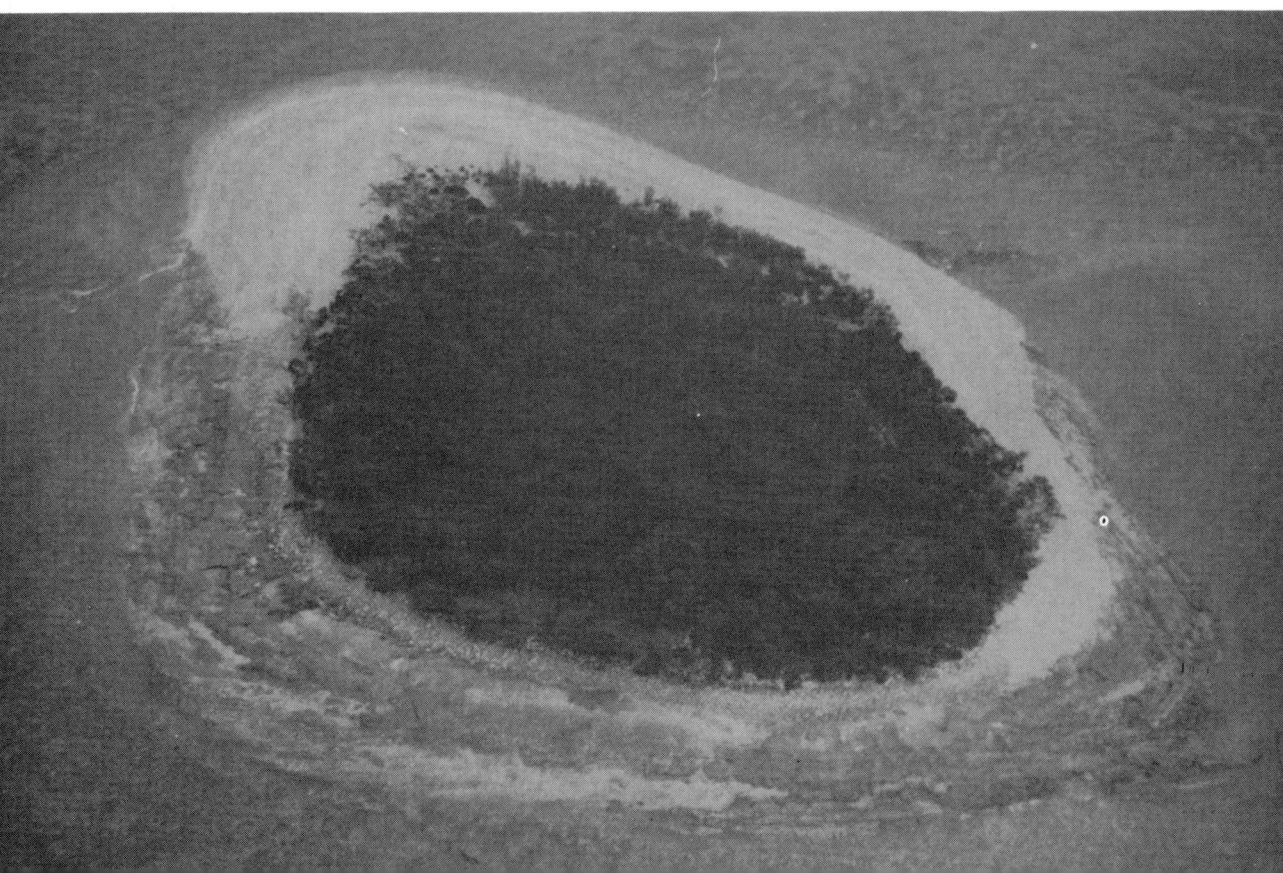

Turtle soup

It was not until 1st July 1923, eighty years after Heron Island was first surveyed, that Mr L. Marsh was granted a lease by the Queensland government to establish a turtle soup factory there. It cost him an annual rental of £10.

Although most turtles are not very palatable, the green turtle is a popular delicacy in some parts of the world. In the 1920s thousands of green turtles, which had been visiting Heron Island each year, had a nasty shock.

In the sea the turtle is in its element and relatively safe. It can glide gracefully or turn and swim very fast. On land, turtles are slow-moving and defenceless. They presented an easy catch for the men who patrolled the beach at night. The men followed the turtle tracks up the beach and turned the turtles on their backs, where they could not right themselves, and left them there until high tide the next day. Then they were taken by boat or punt to a small jetty and transferred to a truck which took them to the factory on the sheltered north-west side of the island.

In a galvanized iron shed the turtles' heads were chopped off and the flippers and breast plate (plastron) were cut away. The flesh and fat were removed and together with the flippers were boiled for eighteen hours. The mixture was then strained into concentrating

13 *A turtle swimming among coral.*

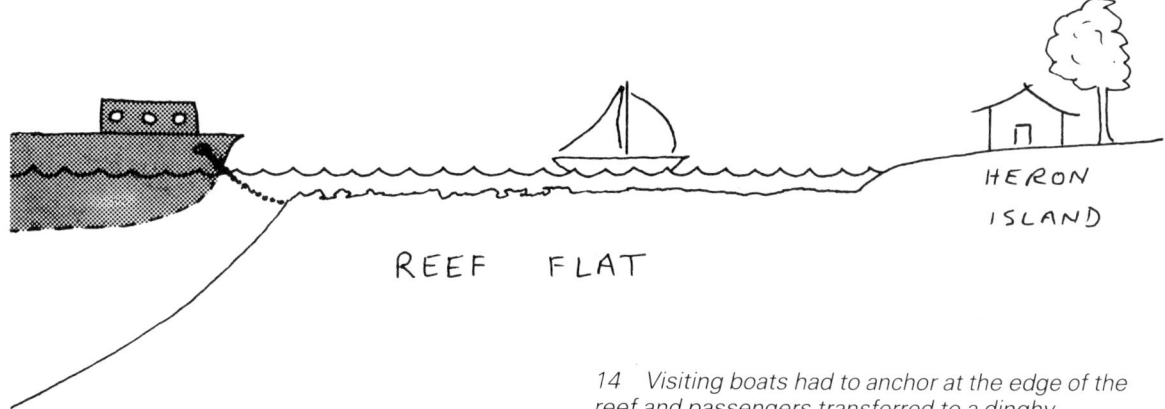

14 Visiting boats had to anchor at the edge of the reef and passengers transferred to a dinghy.

vats in which the liquid was boiled until the soup was dense enough for canning.

By the 1926-27 season the factory was producing about 25,000 tins of soup.

Find out from the information given in chapter 7 how long the turtle season is. Then work out the approximate number of tins produced on average each day.

Why do the turtles make themselves so vulnerable by leaving the sea and coming ashore? Why would it have been better if the men had waited until the turtles were making their way back down the beach before they caught them?

In September 1950 the Queensland government prohibited the taking of green turtles or their eggs in Queensland waters. At last the future looked brighter for the Heron Island turtles.

Early tourists

In the meantime the management of Heron Island changed hands a couple of times but the soup factory did not prosper. In 1932 a Scandinavian, Captain Christian Poulson, rented a part of the island, which was then valued at £90 a year.

Chris Poulson was an excellent sailor and used to make frequent crossings to and from the Australian mainland. Other people had recognized that the islands of the Capricorn Group would be suitable for tourism, but Chris Poulson was the first to do something about it. He began by bringing his friends to Heron Island for a holiday. They stayed in makeshift huts and spent the days swimming, fishing and lazing in the sun.

Poulson improved the facilities and by 1944 had forty cabins, an amenities block and a tennis court.

He named one of his motor boats the *Capre* after his children: Cynthia, Audrey, Pamela, Robert and Eileen. Twice a week the 18-metre *Capre* made the five-hour journey from Gladstone to Heron. The water over the surrounding reef was too shallow for the motor boat so it had to anchor at the edge of the coral platform and the passengers were transferred to a dinghy. Even small boats had to wait until high tide before they could float over the reef. Later a channel was dynamited through the coral and a permanent harbour built.

In 1947 Chris Poulson, in partnership with Captain S. C. Middlemiss, bought three old RAAF Catalina flying boats or sea planes. From these they produced one aircraft which carried twenty-eight passengers. On 12th July 1947 they began to operate a regular service from Brisbane to Heron, with a flying time of two hours ten minutes.

On 28th November of that year tragedy struck; Chris Poulson was lost when his boat disappeared at sea near Heron Island.

New owners

You can own a percentage of a business or company by buying shares in it. At one time Heron Island resort was a business which was partly owned by several different shareholders. In 1973 the shipping company, Peninsula & Orient Australia Limited, acquired a majority of the shares in the resort. In 1980 the company purchased the remaining shares, making it the sole owner. P & O then formed a subsidiary company, Heron Island Proprietary Limited, to run the resort.

Planning a resort

How to transport visitors to the island was just one of the considerations Chris Poulson had to face when developing the resort. Referring to your ideas about establishing a settlement here, list some of the other problems associated with accommodating people on such an island.

Taking into account the points made in the list below, decide how you would turn a beautiful but very small island into a profitable holiday resort.

- The island has no fresh water of its own.
- How can you restrict the amount of water people use?
- One of the reasons visitors come to the island is to see the turtles, fish and birds.
- If you eat them you would decrease the appeal of the island.
- What do you give the guests to eat?
- How would you provide heat for cooking?
- What form of lighting would you use?
- How could you produce electricity? And what are the alternatives?
- What do you do with all the rubbish?
- Can the waste be separated into that which decomposes naturally, such as food scraps, and that which doesn't?
- When promoting holidays on the island, what are the main attractions you can highlight? And why?
- What sort of person do you want to encourage to stay on your island?
- List the different ways in which you can advertise the resort. Explain why some methods are better than others.

In pairs or in two teams, consider two very different types of resort. It is your job to decide how Heron Island should be developed and managed.

Team A wants a resort with a beach dotted with sunshades, a swimming pool with loungers, waiters serving cocktails on the terrace, souvenir shops, video games, plenty of evening entertainment and none of the restrictions imposed in a national park.

Team B wants a resort where guests can appreciate the flora and fauna of the island. Conservation is a major part of the policy and visitors are encouraged to learn about the plants, birds and animals. They can take photos but they cannot collect shells and coral, pick flowers nor go fishing.

There are, of course, many other ways in which Heron Island could have been developed and the above exercise could incorporate several other groups with particular interests. Some people might prefer to leave the island entirely to the birds and turtles, others might want to drill for oil or keep the island as a private retreat for themselves.

Pressure groups are often very single-minded. The final outcome of a planning meeting is likely to be a compromise between conflicting opinions.

Being as imaginative as you like, and given what you already know of Heron Island, draw a plan of the resort, showing in detail how the island *could* be used if you had a completely free hand. You may want to add to this when you have read the rest of the book.

Next choose a suitable magazine in which to advertise the holiday resort you have planned. Design an advertisement which prospective customers will find irresistible.

Now look at it from the visitor's point of view. You are planning a holiday. Write a list of at least six ingredients that make up your ideal holiday. How many of these can be found on Heron Island?

4

What makes the island tick?

Consider what effect the following would have:

- the slaughter of thousands of turtles every year
- constant fishing around the island
- each visitor taking away just one piece of coral
- each visitor discarding one bottle or can on the beach or in the sea
- burning of trees for cooking, campfires, etc.

Protect and thrive

It was not long before people realized that the best long-term interests for Heron Island lay in preserving, rather than destroying, the natural environment. If we do not look after the land it will become useless.

Without a strong emphasis on conservation this small island would soon lose its attraction for the fish, the turtles, the birds and the humans.

With about two hundred people staying on Heron Island at any one time, the natural environment is bound to be affected, however careful you are. Even walking can damage the undergrowth or the coral. Yet destruction can be minimized by acting for the good of the community as a whole. The success of Heron Island lies in the balance between encouraging more people to enjoy the island and ensuring that the environment is not ruined.

As we shall see when we go to the island in the next chapter, the resort itself takes up just one corner of the island. The park rangers and the scientific research station have been allocated other segments, and the rest belongs to the birds and turtles.

Everyone who visits Heron Island is encouraged to maintain a caring approach towards the island and all of its inhabitants. Walks through the woods and out onto the coral reef introduce you to the wildlife, much of which is actually more tame than wild.

No building is higher than two storeys and most of them are designed to blend in with the surroundings. You are urged not to waste water or electricity, which are produced on the island.

15   Coral and other marine life can be easily damaged.

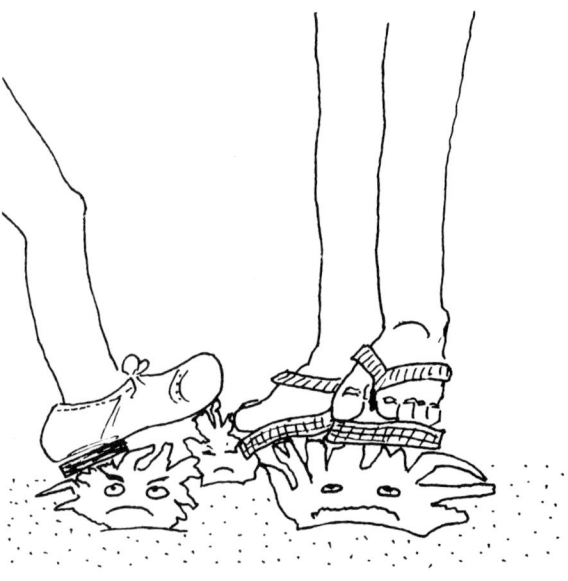

16 Waste collection.

Practical needs

For many people Heron Island is the perfect holiday spot. But even dream islands do not run themselves. The job of providing for everyone's day-to-day needs is a very practical one. How, for example, do you organize the disposal of waste and the delivery of food?

A community of this size produces a lot of waste which has to be disposed of efficiently. Rather than trying to dig a hole in the hard coral and bury the rubbish, the waste is divided into three different types – food, paper, cans – each of which is dealt with separately.

With an eye for economy as well as ecology, can you suggest how each of the three types of waste might be disposed of?

Hank has lived and worked on Heron Island for over twenty-five years. One of his jobs is to ensure that the necessary operation of waste disposal runs smoothly. Anything which is biodegradable is loaded into bins and taken far out into the deep channel, where the seagulls and fish have a feast. Combustible items, such as paper and cardboard, are burned in an incinerator. And non-perishables, such as cans and glass, are taken back to the mainland on the launch.

The island generates its own electricity. The generator produces 360 kilowatts of power which supplies the resort, research station and ranger station. Frank Cobden, the assistant engineer, maintains the generator.

17 A fork-lift truck is used to unload food supplies from the barge and carry the goods across the sandy beach. The boat is called the *Robert Poulson*, after one of Chris Poulson's sons.

18 Frank Cobden checks the oil level of the generator, using a dip stick. ▼

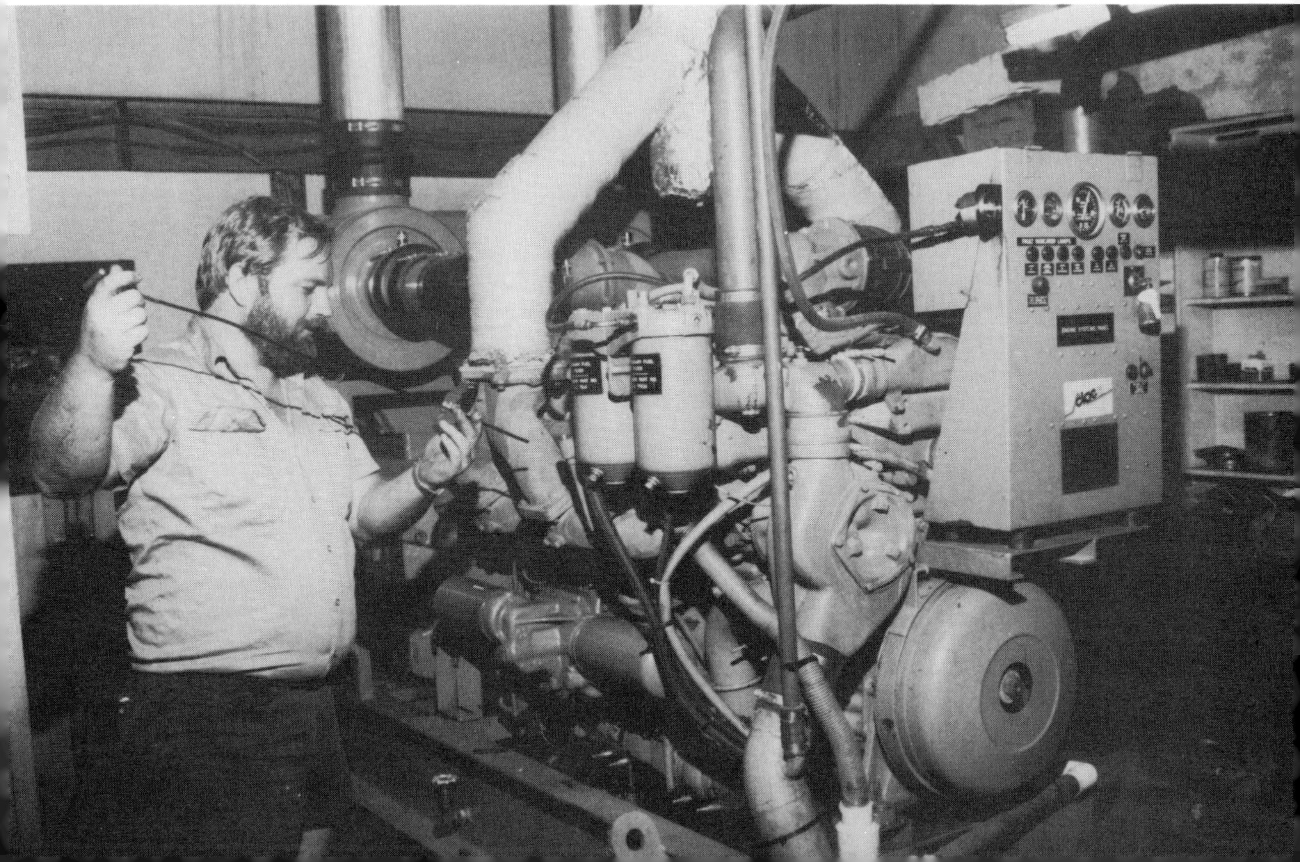

Making drinking water

Because of the great cost of bringing drinking water from Gladstone, a desalination plant has been installed on Heron Island. This purifies sea water by taking out the salt and the impurities. The result is tap water with a salt content no greater than that of Brisbane.

Frank, who looks after the running of the plant, explains how it works: "The sea water is stored in large holding tanks and then filtered through a sand bed to clean out any bits of rubbish. Then it passes through an ultraviolet light filter to kill the bacteria."

In the first photo Frank is topping up the oil in the high-pressure pump. This pump increases the pressure of the water before it passes through a membrane filter to separate the larger salt molecules from the smaller water molecules. On one side of the membrane is the sea water with a high salt content, and on the other side is water with low salinity.

"If you increase the pressure on the salty side", continues Frank, "and keep pumping salt water over the top of the membrane, the salt from the low-salt side moves to the high-salt side. What remains is almost salt-free water."

Making drinking water:
19 Topping up the oil in the high-pressure pump. ▶

20 *Flow meter.* ▼   21 *Pressure valves.* ▶

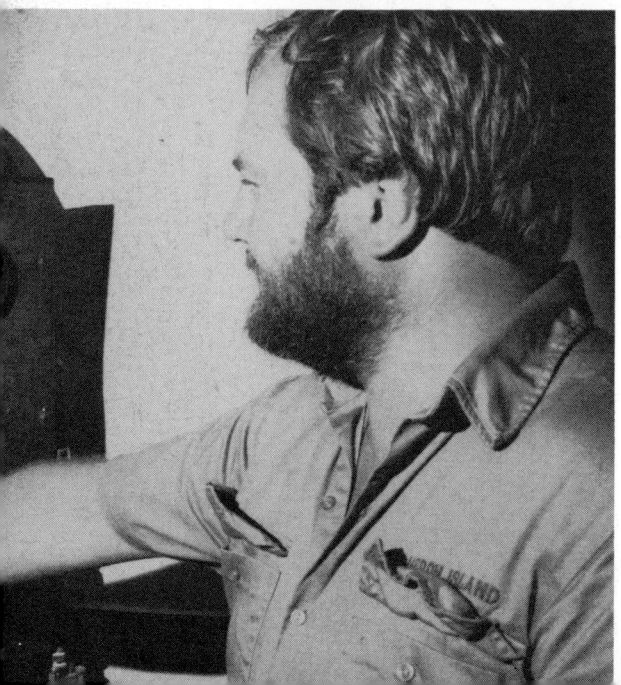

The rate of flow is constantly monitored by a flow meter, and Frank can adjust the water pressure by operating pressure valves.

The plant needs about 50 litres of sea water to produce 8 litres of fresh water every minute from each of four membranes. The daily output is around 40,000 litres. On average, each person on the island uses about 200 litres of desalinated water per day. Rather than using fresh water to flush the toilets, these are on a separate plumbing system and use sea water.

Draw a flow diagram to illustrate all the stages of the desalination process, starting with the sea water in the storage tank and finishing with the distribution of fresh water to the units around the island.

5
The daily round

Your visit to Heron Island begins with a ride in one of three helicopters that shuttle people to and from the island every day. The flight leaves from Gladstone Airport on the Queensland coast.

Helicopter flight

Before you board the helicopter a pouch containing a lifejacket is tied around your waist. You are one of five passengers — two in the front, three in the back.

22 Putting on the pouch containing a lifejacket. ▶

Once you are inside, safety belts are clicked on and the engine starts up. It is so loud that you have headphones to block out the noise and, when you take off, James Bond music drowns out the engine.

23 The helicopter pilot.

24 Some of the instruments on the helicopter control panel.
▼

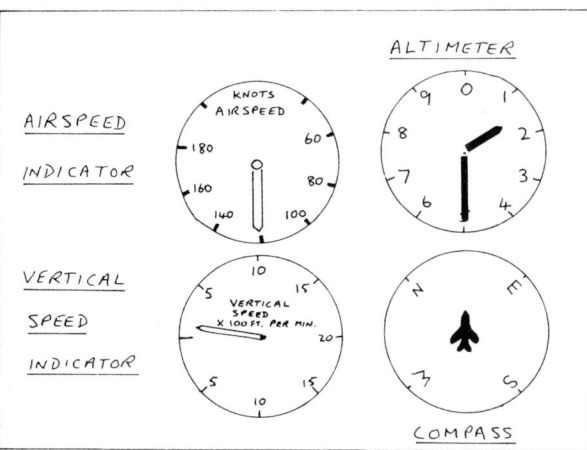

From your vantage point next to the pilot, you can read the instruments. A compass indicates in which direction you are travelling; an altimeter gives your height (the big hand shows hundreds of feet, the small hand shows thousands of feet); an airspeed indicator shows your speed in knots; a vertical speed indicator tells you how fast you are going up or down.

How fast are you flying? And at what height?

Given that 1 knot (nautical mile per hour) is equivalent to 1.15 miles per hour, what is your speed in m.p.h.?

Does the vertical speed indicator show that the helicopter is gaining or losing altitude?

25

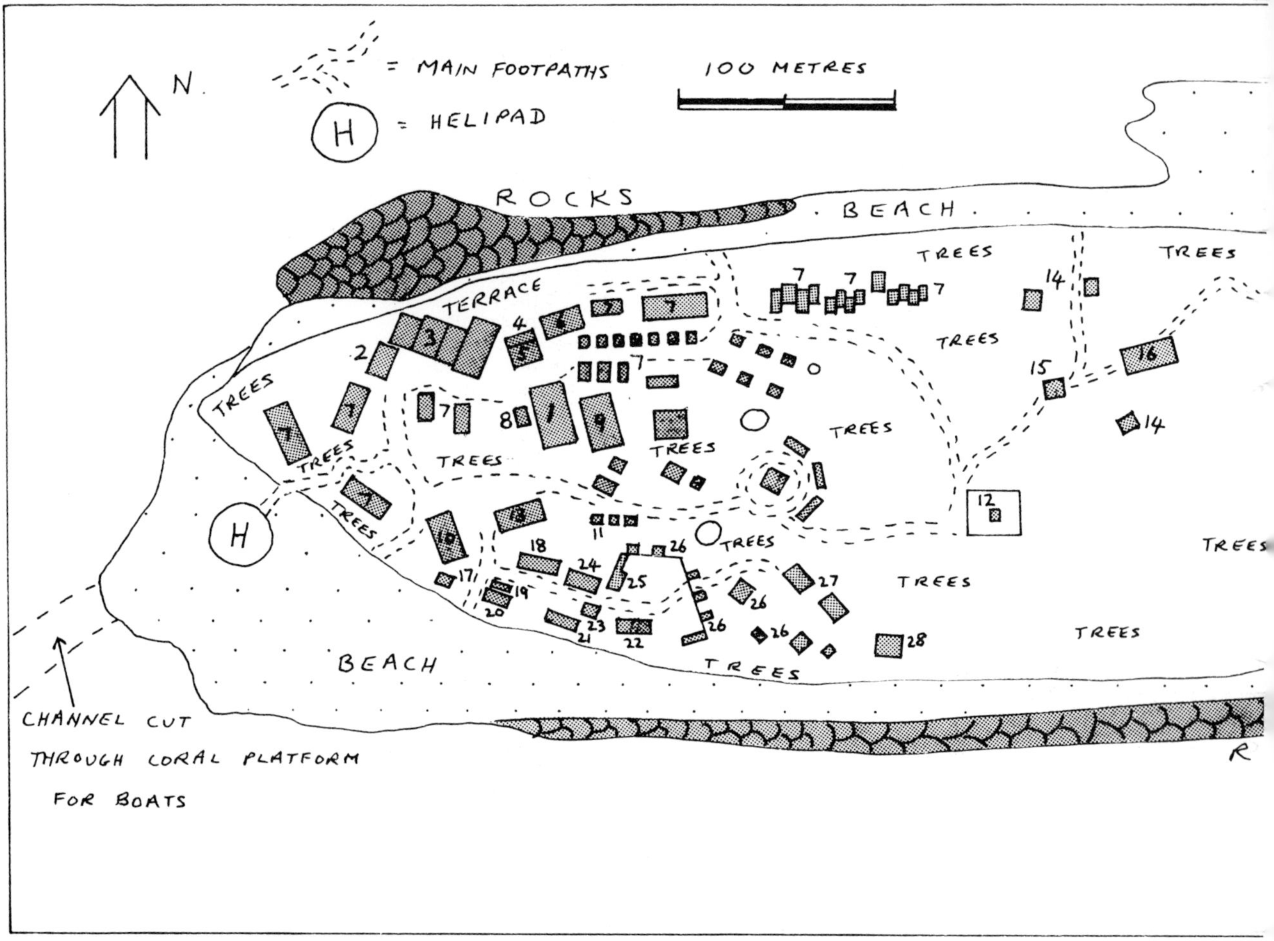

The helicopter flies over patches of turquoise sea. This is your first sight of the coral reef, submerged just below the surface of the water. Then, after twenty minutes in the air, the pilot points ahead. In the middle of one ring of mottled coral is a green saucer of land, fringed with white sand.

An old shipwreck juts out of the water at one end of Heron Reef. Nearby, a channel of dark blue cuts through the coral from the open sea to a jetty, where three boats are moored.

The island itself is covered with trees, and several small buildings are just visible between them. A circle of concrete on the beach is the landing pad. Touch-down is smooth . . . you have arrived on Heron Island.

A cheaper way to travel to Heron Island is by the launch *Wave Piercer*. It takes over an hour and carries 120 people who are treated to a video film about the island and its approach to conservation.

25 *Your welcome to the island.*

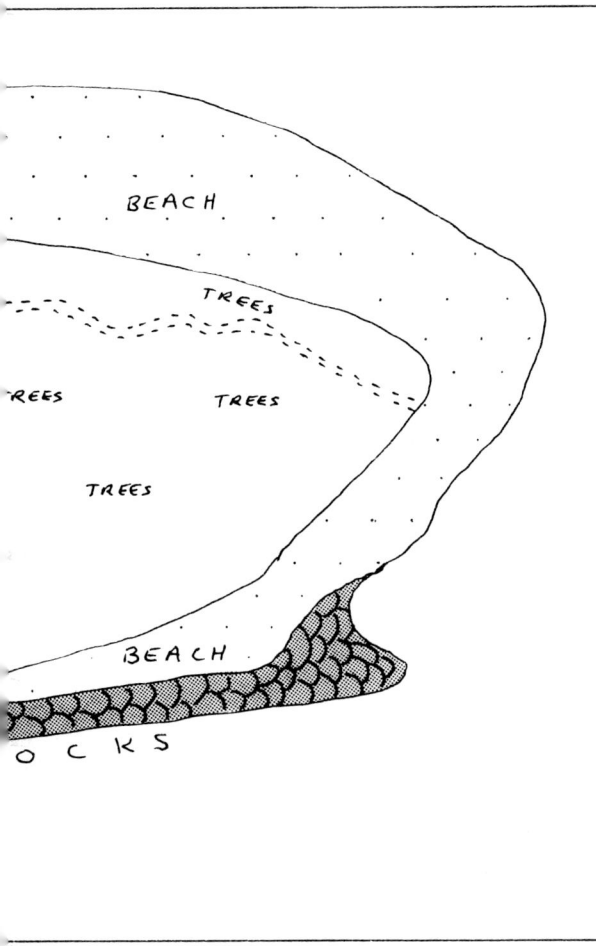

26 Plan of Heron Island.

Key

Resort amenities

1 Dining room
2 Reception and manager's office
3 Commonroom and bar
4 Dive shop
5 Gift shop
6 Interpretive centre
7 Bedrooms
8 Swimming pool
9 Tennis court
10 Powerhouse
11 Staff quarters
12 Garbage disposal
13 Workshops

National Parks & Wildlife Service amenities

14 Shelter sheds
15 Workshop
16 Accommodation and office

Research Station amenities

17 Maintenance officer's residence
18 Workshop and boatshed
19 Staff laundry and store
20 Reception and office
21 Teaching laboratory
22 Laboratory
23 Aquarium
24 Visitors' dining room
25 Ablutions block
26 Cabins
27 Houses
28 Director's residence

A warm welcome

After everyone has been welcomed, you are taken on a guided tour of the resort by one of the staff, called an *interpretive*. It is the job of the interpretives to help visitors appreciate all aspects of the island.

It's hard to take it all in at first; the buildings seem to be scattered around in no logical order. From the helipad the group is led inland along a sandy track. A few trees provide some welcome shade from the glaring midday sun. What are the buildings on either side of you?

When you turn left, in which direction are you facing?

After about 50 metres you reach the administrative block. This is where you come to sort out any problems and confirm your departure time at the end of your stay.

The manager comes out of his office and explains his role: "I make sure the staff help our visitors get the most out of their holiday here. People want value for money, so the food must be good, the rooms comfortable and all the facilities functioning well."

Next to the office is the bar and commonroom, an ideal place to escape from the heat of the sun, and play cards, chess or table tennis.

You go through the commonroom to the terrace, an open-air bar and café which would not look out of place in the south of France. The terrace is where many guests meet, especially after a tiring day, to relax, chat and watch the sunset. Is this the best place to sit and watch the sun setting? Why?

From here the interpretive takes the group to

the dive centre, where scuba gear can be rented and qualified divers can sign up to go out on one of the dive boats.

Next-door is the gift shop which sells T-shirts, sunglasses, sunhats, suntan lotion, maps, posters and souvenirs.

Heading south you soon reach the swimming pool, just outside the dining room. Suggest reasons why there should be a swimming pool when the sea is so close.

Then, walking past the northern end of the dining room, you see the interpretive centre on your left. The centre has maps, sketches, photos and samples of the coral reef. The displays illustrate the web of life which is busily minding its own business just a few metres away.

Eventually you are taken to your room where your bags are waiting for you. Before you go any further, work out from the map the total distance you have walked so far. This can be done very roughly by following the route with a ruler. A more accurate method is to take a piece of cotton or thin string and lay it along the entire route. Then straighten it out and measure the length of string used against a ruler.

Room number 20 is a chalet which you are sharing with a friend. The room is simple and comfortable, rather than luxurious: two beds, two wardrobes, a washbasin and mirror. There's a kettle on the sideboard, with coffee and tea bags, so you can make yourself a cuppa at any time. The water tastes a little salty, and, remembering what you have read about the desalination plant, you know why.

It's lunchtime. Looking at the layout of the resort, you see the dining room is only 30 or 40 metres away.

"For me it's a holiday job," says one of the waiters. "I'm nineteen and will be going back to college in Brisbane in two weeks. I used to clean rooms and make beds, but it's more fun serving in the dining room and chatting with the guests."

27 Lunchtime.

Lunch is a buffet, with a large spread of different seafoods, meat, vegetables, salads and desserts.

After eating more than you should have done, you stroll over to the notice board outside the shop to see what activities are planned.

ACTIVITIES INFORMATION
Wednesday, 20th

Island Walk: Meet Janine outside the Gift Shop at 4.00 pm for a guided walk to learn about the island's history, birds, turtles and trees.

Snorkel Lesson: Janine will meet you at the pool at 10.30 am to show you the correct use of fins, mask and snorkel. Please have the gear with you.

Yellow Sub: The Yellow Submarine will depart the harbour at 9.00 and 2.00. Please book at the Gift Shop and be at the harbour 10 minutes before departure.

Reef Walk: Cary will conduct a guided reef walk at 3.00 pm. The walk is very informative as we show you varied marine life on Heron Reef. You may borrow sand shoes and reef sticks – both very necessary. Meet on the Terrace outside the common-room.

Dive Boat: Our dive boats depart the harbour twice daily. We take qualified divers and snorkellers to various dive locations. The boats depart at 9.15 am and 2.15 pm. Please book at the Dive Shop and be at the harbour with all your gear 10 minutes before departure.

☆ ☆ EVENING ENTERTAINMENT ☆ ☆

FILM "Wonders of the reef"

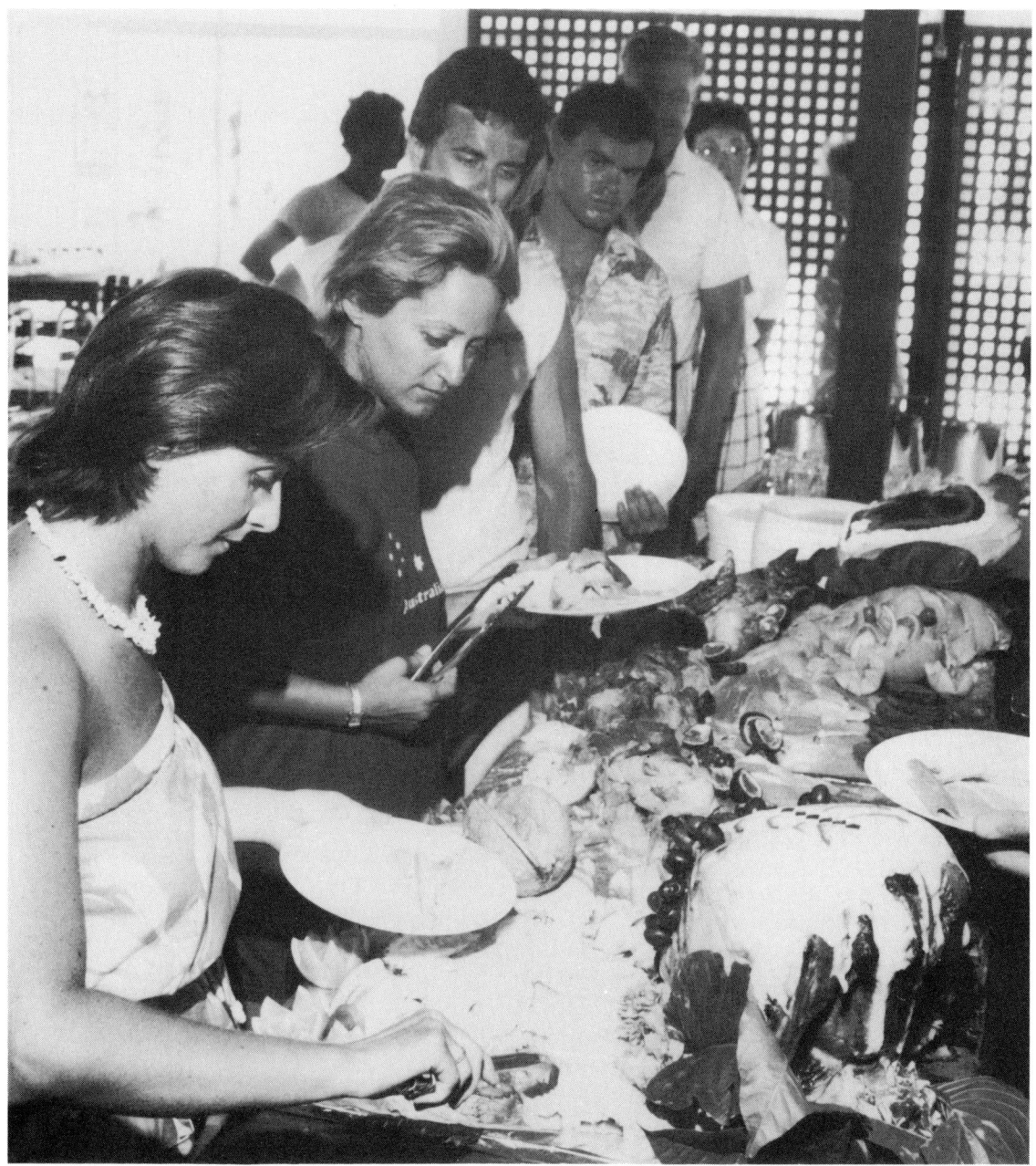

This morning they had snorkel lessons in the pool for novices, while the experts went out scuba diving on the reef.

At 2.15 this afternoon the scuba divers will take a boat out to a different dive site. At 3.00 pm there's a reef walk led by one of the staff. The Yellow Sub sounds intriguing; you make a mental note to ask someone about that.

You don't want to do anything too energetic on your first day. Already you are finding that you have to drink more because your body has become dehydrated by the sun and the heat. Just being out in the sunshine for long periods can be quite exhausting.

At 4.00 pm there's an island walk. Then, after dinner this evening, a film will be shown in the commonroom. Most evenings there are films or talks about the marine life of the reef, conservation, green turtles or the birds of Heron Island.

DINNER
WEDNESDAY, 20th

SOUP

ENTREE

MINI SPRING ROLLS
OR
MELON WITH GAMMON

MAIN COURSE

SEA PERCH GRENOBLOISE
fillets of boneless sea perch grilled in butter
with lemon juice

WIENER SCHNITZEL PROVENCALE
pink veal steak crumbed and pan fried, topped
with cheese and fresh tomato puree

PORK LOIN ROBERY
baked loin of pork sliced, served with light
mustard sauce, steamed apples and
cranberries

VEGETABLES
roast potatoes, glazed carrots, French beans
OR
SALADS

DESSERTS
baked apple with custard
peach melba
OR
CHEESE AND FRUITS

In many ways Heron Island is a sand-between-the-toes resort, with few of the luxuries you find in top international hotels. Yet it's a place where you can rough it in style when it comes to eating.

If you were a food correspondent for a magazine or radio programme, how would you describe the dinner shown in the menu above? Use your imagination to give the readers or listeners the impression that they are actually there enjoying the meal.

The island's visitors

A visit to Heron Island is not cheap, especially if your journey began on the other side of the world. Nearly everything on the island has to be imported from the mainland, and that adds to the expense.

Visitors from abroad have to travel a long way to reach the island. It is approximately 310 miles from Brisbane (Australia), 1,730 miles from Auckland (New Zealand), 4,120 miles from Tokyo (Japan), 7,500 miles from San Francisco (USA), and 10,600 miles from London (England).

Using the figures below, draw two different types of graph to show where visitors to Heron Island come from. One graph should illustrate the percentage figures given. The other should show the actual numbers of visitors from each country when the total number of visitors is 10,000 in one year.

Australia	35%
USA and Canada	33%
Germany	11%
Britain	8%
Scandinavia	4%
Japan	4%
New Zealand	3%
Others	2%

Most of those who come from outside Australia combine a visit to Heron Island with other stops around Australia. Many visitors have spent some time in Sydney, perhaps on business or going to a performance at the Opera House. Some have been sailing around other islands of the Great Barrier Reef, or deep-sea fishing out of Cairns in northern Queensland. And others have ventured into the heart of the Australian Outback, where they have climbed Ayers Rock, one of Australia's famous landmarks. But when it comes to getting close to nature, Heron Island is most people's first choice.

6

Life on land

"I'm your guide today," says Janine. "We're going to spend about two hours walking slowly across the island and I'll tell you some of the unusual facts about the inhabitants."

The island walk begins outside the gift shop at 4.00 pm. Janine is a member of the interpretive staff and knows the island well. She leads the group on rough, meandering tracks through dense woodland and introduces you to the bird and plant life.

"This is where everyone becomes an instant zoologist and botanist and you'll soon appreciate that Heron Island has lots of extraordinary visitors besides the resort guests!"

Janine explains how important it is not to disturb or interfere with the bird life. Yet even with strict rules on conservation, having so many people on such a small island inevitably changes the course of nature. The island has lost its ground-nesting birds and the grey-tailed tattler is dying out.

The behaviour of the land-rails is very different depending on which end of the island they live on. Those near the resort are quite tame and will even walk into your room, whereas those deep in the woods run away as soon as they see you coming.

All visitors are asked to "Take only photographs and notes, leave only footprints".

The island is free from plants that scratch or sting and there are no poisonous reptiles or insects.

Over fifty species of birds have been seen on Heron Island; thirty of them are regulars. Most of the birds are aquatic animals, which means that they look to the sea for their food.

Noddy terns

The white-capped noddy terns (*Anous minutus*) seem to be everywhere – an

28 *Pisonia tree full of noddy terns.*

estimated 20,000 of them. Sometimes a hundred noddy terns will roost on one pisonia tree. They fill the trees all around the resort and have some very strange habits. They spend much of their time nodding to their mate and apparently agreeing all the time, yet when it comes to building the nest, it's a very different story.

Janine describes the nest-building procedure: "The female tern sits on a suitable branch and sends the male off to look for the first leaf to build their nest. When he returns with a leaf she inspects it with her beak — is it too dry or too damp? Then she nearly always rejects it and he has to go looking for another.

29 *A noddy tern on her nest.*

This may be repeated half a dozen or more times depending on how rebellious she feels. When she eventually approves the first leaf, life becomes easier and she is no longer so particular."

The nest is made mostly of pisonia leaves glued together with guano. It is almost flat and provides a precarious platform for the eggs and chicks. If they fall they are abandoned and the terns usually lay another egg.

The noddy terns live on Heron Island throughout the year. Their nesting season extends from September to December and most of the eggs hatch in early summer (November and December).

In the early morning both the adults and the young leave the island to go fishing. They feed by skimming over the surface of the water and catching small fish. The young return in the afternoon and the adults come back just before dark.

They are a sooty black colour all over except for the white cap. The main enemy of the noddy terns is the violent tropical storm which, although infrequent, can kill large numbers. Also, the sticky seeds of the pisonia tree can cling to the birds' feathers. If too many seeds attach themselves the birds cannot fly in search of food and so they die. "This is an example of when you should let nature take its course," says Janine. "Don't try to pull the seeds off; you'll probably cause the bird more pain."

Mutton birds

The funniest bird on Heron Island must be the wedge-tailed shearwater (*Puffinus pacificus*). It is dark brown with a dark, downward-hooked beak and pink feet. It is usually called a mutton bird because it is said to taste like mutton.

Some 16,000 mutton birds nest here after making a 12,500-mile journey to escape the Siberian winter. Each year they return to the same nesting site. They live on the island from October to May.

Although very good at flying and navigating, they are comically inept at taking off and landing. Because of their large wingspan and restricted take-off area, they run along a path as fast as they can and launch themselves in an opening in the vegetation.

Lacking any grace or style, they land pancake fashion as near to their burrow as possible. When resting on land they fold their legs and wings and sit with the body directly on the ground, not standing as other birds do.

30   *A wedge-tailed shearwater or mutton bird resting on the ground.*

While the adults are courting during the night, newcomers to the island are kept awake by chilling, childlike cries which sound like a cross between babies wailing and a walrus with asthma.

The mutton bird makes its nest by burrowing into the ground around the gnarled roots of a pisonia tree. Heron Island is honeycombed with mutton bird tunnels which may be up to 3m long. The nesting chamber is lined with grass, and a single egg is incubated by both adults.

At first light the adult not incubating the egg leaves the island to collect fish, then returns in the evening. Once the baby is hatched the adult brings food home from its fishing trips to feed the chick at night.

When the chick has been fattened up so much that it is larger than the adult, the parents abandon it before it has learned to fly. The fledglings are self-taught flyers and their first attempts are especially clumsy.

"You have to keep your wits about you in the evenings," explains Janine. "Fledgling mutton birds charge along the paths trying to get airborne. Those that manage to take off forget to steer and usually crash into a tree or building. They slide to the ground and are stunned at first, but their fat, fleshy bodies protect them from serious harm and they soon get up, shake themselves and try again."

Most of the wedge-tailed shearwaters have left Heron Island by April or May and find their own way half way round the world to Siberia.

During which months should you visit Heron Island to see:
(a) noddy terns making their nests?
(b) mutton birds learning to fly?

Herons

The reef heron (*Egretta sacra*) which gave its name to the island is resident throughout the year. It has a long, pointed bill, long, yellow-green legs and feet, and a short tail. The heron may be either grey or white. It stretches its long neck to catch food and folds it into an S-shape when in flight. It builds a nest of twigs and small branches in the pandanus trees. During low tide it fishes in the coral pools and on the reef flat for small crustaceans, fish and molluscs. About 300 herons are resident here.

Gulls

The silver gull (*Larus novaehollandiae*) is almost entirely white with black wing tips. Its white eyes are ringed with red. About 500 of the gulls base themselves on Heron Island.

Visitors to the island can study bird behaviour all around them. You can watch an interesting sequence of ground displays by the silver gull.

31 Four positions of the silver gull.

(a) When he is standing his ground he adopts the upright threat posture.

(b) In a similar position, but his beak wide open, he delivers a piercing alarm call.

(c) The alarm call accompanied by ducking and hunching movements often ends with an attack, with the head lowered.

(d) The young use this hunched posture when begging for food. Adults use it as a part of the challenge display.

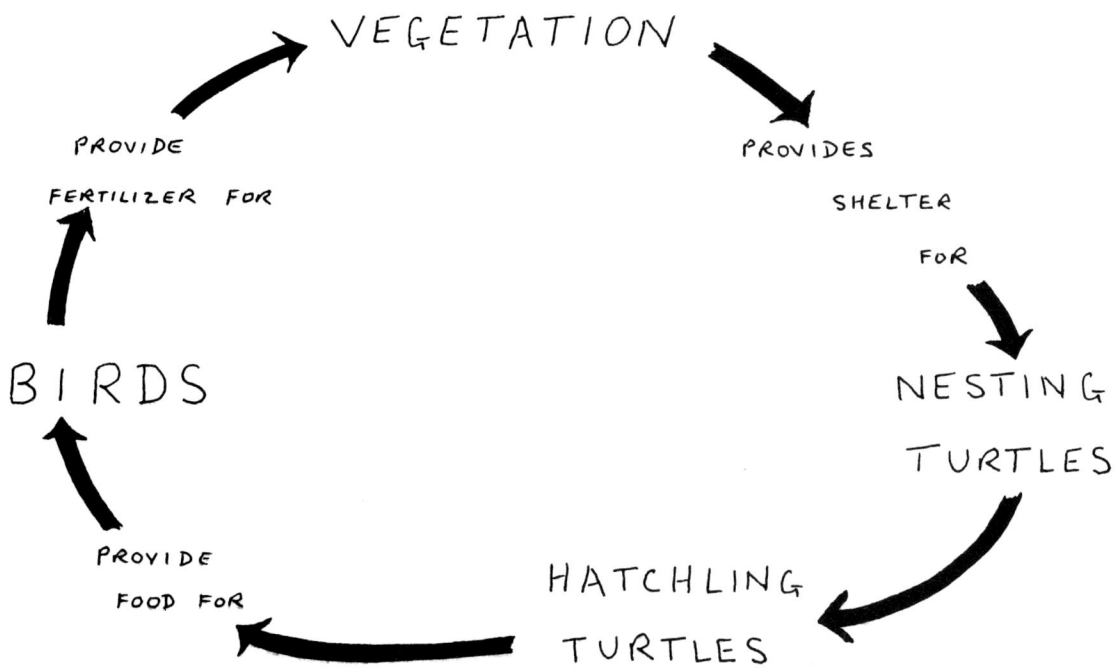

32 *A small part of the web of life on Heron Island.*

From the figures given in the descriptions, draw a graph to show numbers of noddy terns, mutton birds, reef herons and silver gulls on Heron Island.

Rails

The banded land-rail (*Rallus philippensis*) is a walking bird that lives in the thick vegetation of the interior of the island, often near the busiest thoroughfares. It can fly but does not bother, as there are no predators on the island to escape from. The bird is similar to a quail, with a short tail that it often flicks up and down.

"They have adapted to man by accepting any food on offer," explains Janine. "Some will trot right into the dining room. We had one land-rail which had lost a leg, so we named it 'monorail'."

Other birds you are likely to see on Heron Island include bar-shouldered doves, black-naped terns, silver eyes, cormorants, gannets, frigate birds and oystercatchers.

The web of life

A complex pattern of relationships exists between the birds and the plant life of Heron Island. A threat to one species may well endanger another. The vegetation helps to bind the sand together and protect it from the wind. The cay offers a sheltered nesting ground for turtles. Hatchling turtles provide a seasonal delicacy for the birds. Trees and undergrowth give shelter and nesting sites for the birds. The birds, in turn, convert sea food into fertilizer, which nourishes the vegetation.

Vegetation

Pisonia trees cover much of the island. They grow to heights of up to 20m and have a rough, mottled grey trunk and branches. Although they look strong, the timber is soft and brittle.

Casuarinas or she-oaks and pandanus palms

fringe the island. The pandanus has tufted leaves and stilt-like prop roots which form a pyramid of flying buttresses.

The sections of the island which have not been cleared for building are covered with an undergrowth of silver-leaved tournefortia and scaevola bushes.

33 *Inspecting the prop roots of a pandanus palm.*

A carpet of coarse grass and goat's foot convolvulus grows on the higher limits of the beach where the turtles come to lay their eggs. Ah yes, the turtles. They deserve a whole chapter to themselves...

7

The green turtle

There are fewer than thirty places in the world that green turtles (*Chelonia mydas*) consider good enough and clean enough to have their young. The Capricorn Group of islands is the most popular of all of them.

Although turtles are sea creatures they descended from land-living reptiles. Their ancestors left the land and adapted to the sea in all but their method of reproduction. Today, when the turtles drag themselves up the beach to lay their eggs, they are responding to primeval instinct which calls them back to dry land.

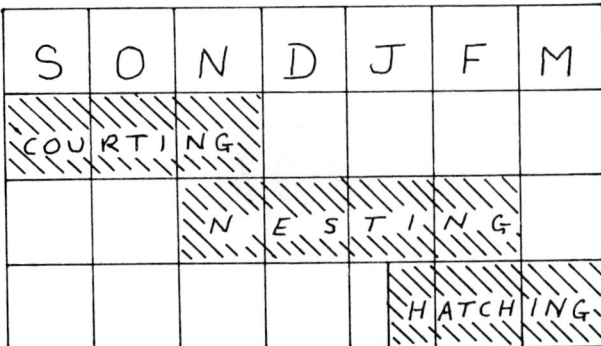

34 Turtle's nesting calendar.

One of the lasting memories of a visit to Heron Island between November and February is the sight of a turtle laying her eggs. Female turtles struggle up the beach at night, usually when the tide is high so that they can swim over the reef platform. This is one occasion when you don't object to being woken at three or four o'clock in the morning.

Egg-laying

Word is out that a large green turtle is lumbering up the beach just 50 metres from the resort. About thirty bleary-eyed people gather round the reptile. They take the lead from Phil Reed who is a park ranger studying turtle behaviour on Heron Island.

The onlookers keep their distance and speak in hushed voices. All torches are switched off. Adult turtles are timid and can easily be

> **How to find nesting turtles**
>
> • Walk along the beach at about high tide mark, looking for turtle tracks. These are about one metre wide.
> • Lights can disturb turtles so keep lights off while walking along the beach. Turtle tracks are easily seen without lights.
> • Follow the tracks carefully and quietly up on to the dune to locate the turtle. Try to avoid excess movement, especially in front of the turtle.
> • Wait quietly, sitting behind the turtle until she has started laying her eggs, i.e. when she is sitting still after a long period of throwing sand. Once the turtle is actually laying she is not normally disturbed by lights, gentle touching or noise.
> • Dig out gently behind the turtle to observe the eggs as they drop. Now is the time to turn on your lights to examine the turtle closely.

ONE METRE

35 Green turtle digging an egg chamber.
36 Newly laid turtle eggs.

disturbed at any stage from leaving the water until well into the process of laying the eggs.

First the turtle finds a suitable location above the high water mark, at the point where the vegetation begins. Then she sets to work scraping away loose sand with all four powerful flippers, to form a shallow body pit. Next, with her hind flippers, she starts to excavate the vertical hole of the egg chamber. She scoops the sand out by the flipperful and deposits it on the ground beside the hole.

Rest stops are frequent. At the end of each rest the turtle raises her head and breathes out noisily, then gulps air into her lungs.

Further down the beach are more tracks and several more females preparing to lay.

After five minutes of laborious shovelling, she stops and, for some reason, changes her mind. She leaves the hollow, heaves her body a couple of metres along the beach and starts digging again. Perhaps something disturbed her, perhaps the ground was too moist or too dry.

Your patient vigil continues for almost an hour as the turtle completes the second excavation. She does not look around to inspect the nest, but when she senses that it is deep enough (about 40cm), she begins laying white, leathery eggs, which look like ping-pong balls.

No stopping her now

The ranger turns on his torch and says it is now

safe to take flash photographs. He gently pulls one of the hind flippers to one side to reveal a small clutch of eggs. Each egg is covered with mucus which protects it from fungal infection. He carefully picks up one of the eggs and passes it round the group. The shell has not yet hardened and feels like soft parchment. It weighs about 20 grams.

Thirty minutes later the turtle has produced over a hundred eggs and the laying is finished. Green turtles have been known to lay over 200 eggs in one clutch.

After filling the egg chamber with sand, the turtle disguises the site by moving forward, extending the position of the body pit. By the time she has done this it is very difficult to see where the eggs are buried. On the mainland of Australia, predators such as lizards, foxes and pigs can detect the nests by their smell, but Heron Island has no such animals.

The turtle then returns to the sea, about four hours after leaving it. She never sees her eggs nor her hatchlings.

37 *Phil and the turtle.*

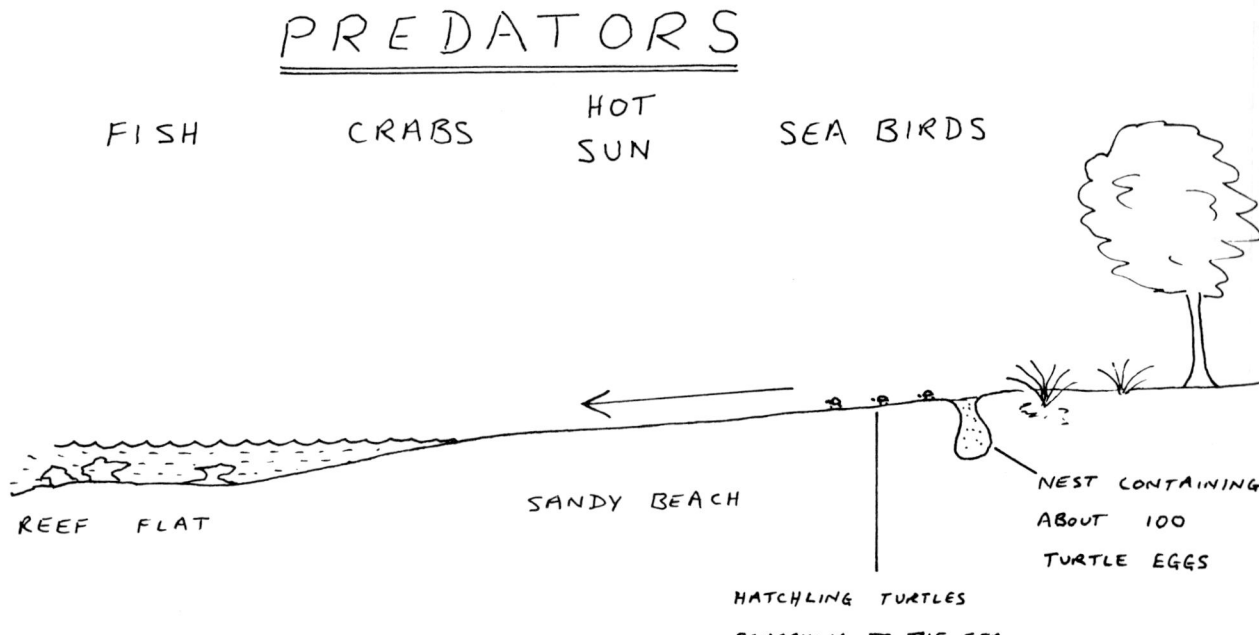

38 Hatchlings have many predators.

In two weeks she will return and lay another clutch. She may lay eight or nine clutches in one season, then wait for four to six years before nesting again.

Is it a boy or a girl?

The eggs are incubated by the warmth of the sand and take an average of nine weeks to hatch. The temperature of the sand determines whether the hatchlings are male or female. On a relatively cool beach, with temperatures between 26° and 28°C, the turtles will all be male. On a warm beach, 32°-34°C, they will be female. Just one very hot day during the incubation period will make them all female. Heron Island is a "cool" beach and so produces an excess of males.

Running the gauntlet

Any time from mid-January to late March the hatchlings fight their way up through the sand. They emerge from their nests to make their instinctive scuttle to the sea. They come out in the evening between about 5pm and midnight.

Under cover of darkness the danger of being eaten is at its lowest, although the baby turtles are still likely to be snapped up by a sea bird or crab. Even those that reach the sea usually provide a meal for the fish, especially in the shallow section over the reef flats.

By moving at night the hatchlings avoid the exhausting effects of the hot sun. But at night they can become disorientated by the lights of the resort and head for those instead of the sea. Guests at the resort are asked to switch off lights which are not in use, not only to save electricity but to save the turtles.

Hatchlings that wander away from the sea become trapped in vegetation and die. Probably fewer than two or three hatchlings from each clutch will survive to reach maturity.

39 A one-day-old turtle. ▶

The growing years

Green turtles live in the open sea and sleep in sheltered parts of the reef, such as in caves or under overhanging ledges, facing inwards.

They are omnivorous for the first year or so of their lives, when they eat marine algae, grasses and jellyfish. Then they turn herbivorous and eat sea grass and other vegetation.

Those that nest on Heron Island swim to feeding grounds in the shallow waters of the continental shelf off the coast of northern Queensland or around the Solomon Islands and New Caledonia. The land near the feeding sites is not suitable for egg-laying because the shore is rocky or edged by mangrove swamps.

Using a little-understood technique of underwater navigation the turtles arrive at the Capricorn Group. They may use a combination of smell and the position of the sun to find their way.

From the map, work out how far the turtles have to swim to their nesting ground.

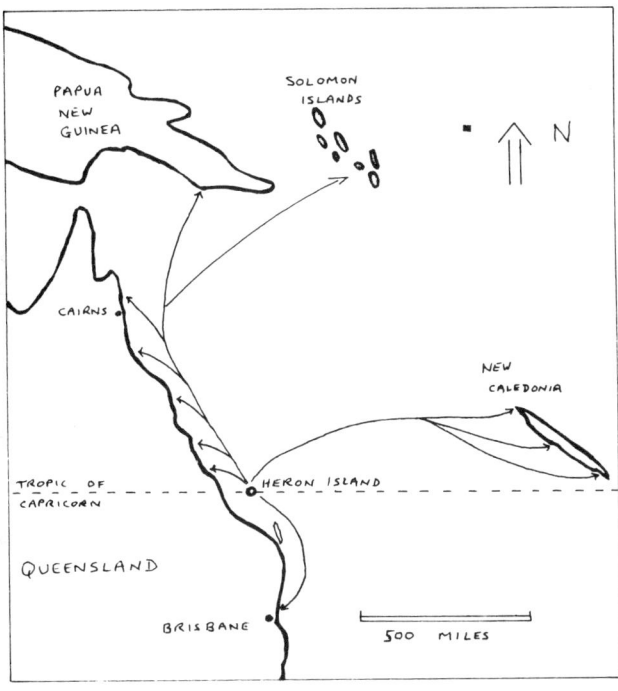

40 Migration routes of green turtles tagged on Heron Island.

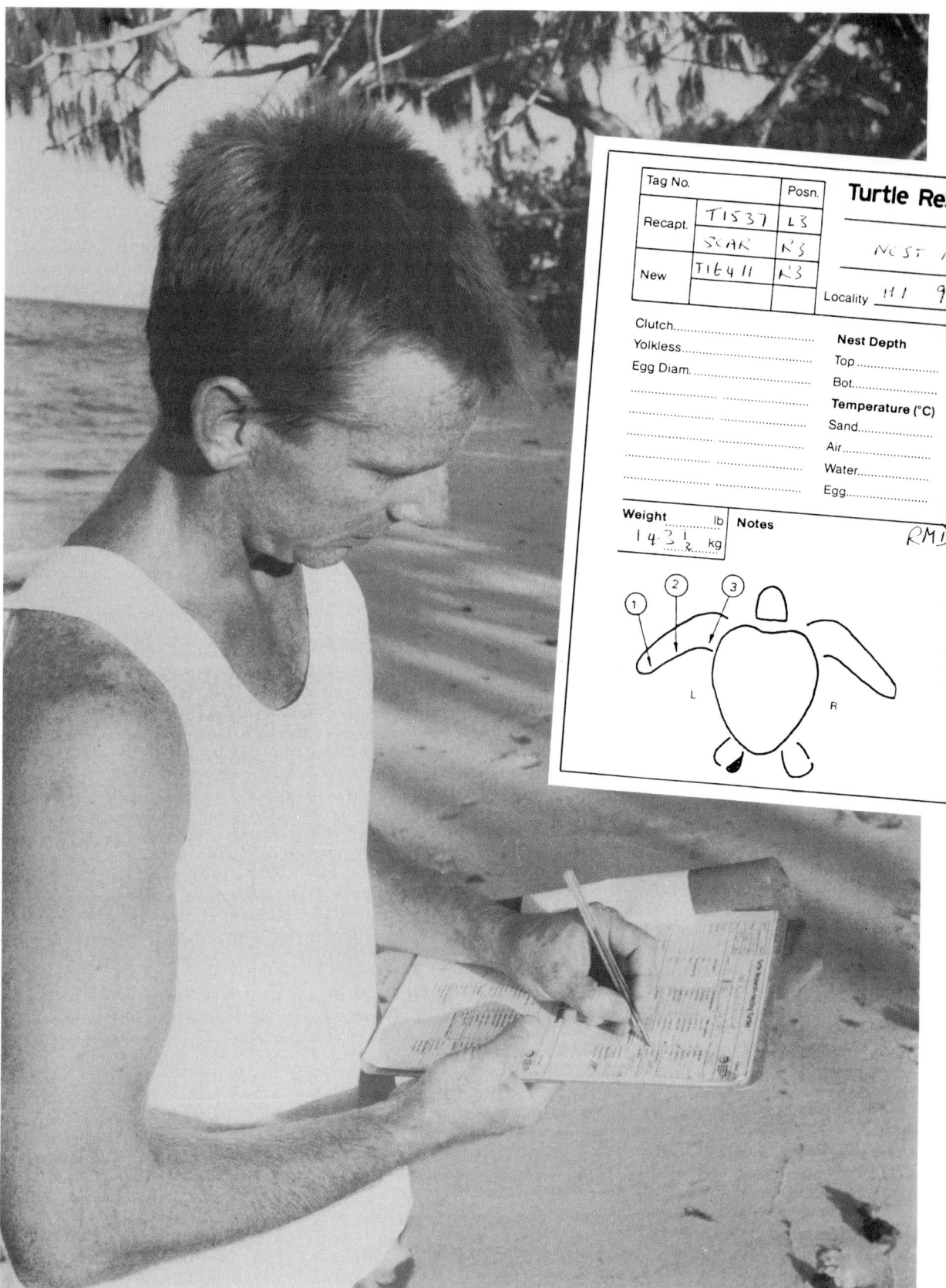

◀ 41 Phil recording details about the turtle.

42 The form he filled in.

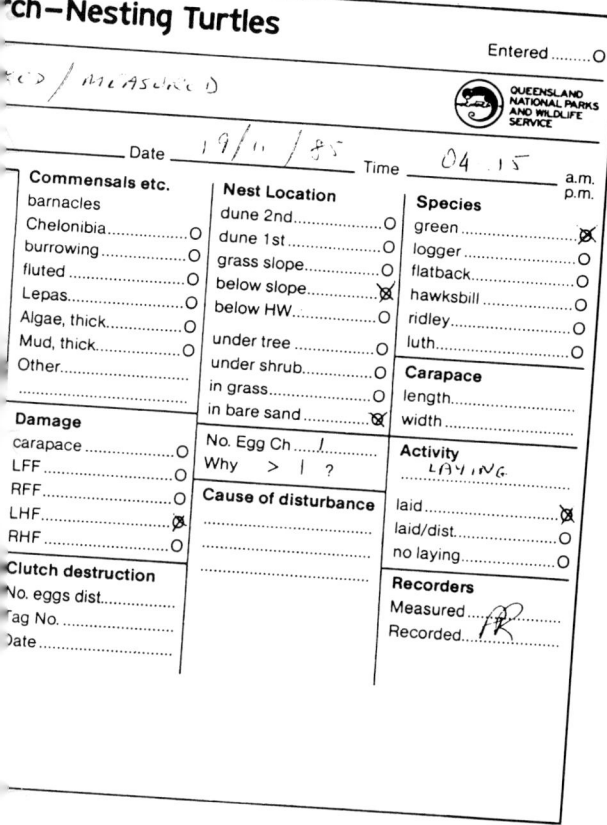

Queensland which are currently being intensively studied by the Queensland National Parks and Wildlife Service. Many students and other volunteers help with the work. Each nestling turtle is tagged on the front flipper so that it can be identified in future.

At peak season over 50 females come ashore to nest every night. The numbers vary enormously from year to year; one year perhaps only 20 turtles and the next as many as 1,500 may be recorded during the nesting season.

A male turtle may never leave the water in his entire life.

The world's turtles

Loggerhead and hawksbill turtles also nest on Heron Island, but not in such great numbers as the green turtles. There are a total of seven species of sea turtle throughout the world. Six are found in Australian waters, and one of them, the flatback turtle, breeds *only* in Australia.

Until recent years the Great Barrier Reef has been difficult to reach. Its isolation has helped save the turtle from being exploited on a vast scale. Although the flesh of the green turtle is considered ideal for soup, and although Heron Island was once a turtle soup factory, the emphasis throughout the whole region has now changed and the turtle is protected. This is not the case in many other areas of the world. The green turtle populations around the Bahamas, Florida, the Dry Tortugas and the Cayman Islands in the Caribbean have been seriously depleted. Once-thriving green turtle rookeries on the islands of Aldabra and the Seychelles in the Indian Ocean have been virtually exterminated.

Turtle oil is now used for cosmetics, the skin is used to make leather goods and the meat is eaten in restaurants.

Compose a letter to a restaurant where turtle soup is served, or to a fishery department currently engaged in catching turtles, expressing your views on the matter.

Weights and measures

Sea turtles usually weigh between 90kg and 140kg. Their shell or carapace is about 100cm long. The smallest green turtle measured on Heron Island had a 91cm carapace and weighed about 80kg. The largest measured 126cm and weighed more than 200kg.

Adult turtles are resilient creatures and, because their blood clots very quickly, they can often survive attacks by predators such as tiger sharks or the great white shark.

Research suggests that a turtle does not start breeding until she is fifty years old. Heron Island is one of two turtle rookeries in

8
Reef life

The resort produces a leaflet which advises guests how to treat the coral during a reef walk:

"Visitors are asked to avoid walking on the living corals, many of which grow less than 1cm per year. All reef walkers should wear protective footwear and use a reef walking stick (useful in keeping one's balance). The best time to begin a reef walk is approximately one hour before low tide. In this way the enthusiast will not end up walking back waist-deep in the incoming tide." The reef is more exposed during the very low tides which can come with the new and full moon.

Walking on the reef

Cary is our guide for the reef walk. "With reef walks taking place nearly every day some of the coral is inevitably broken, but minimise the

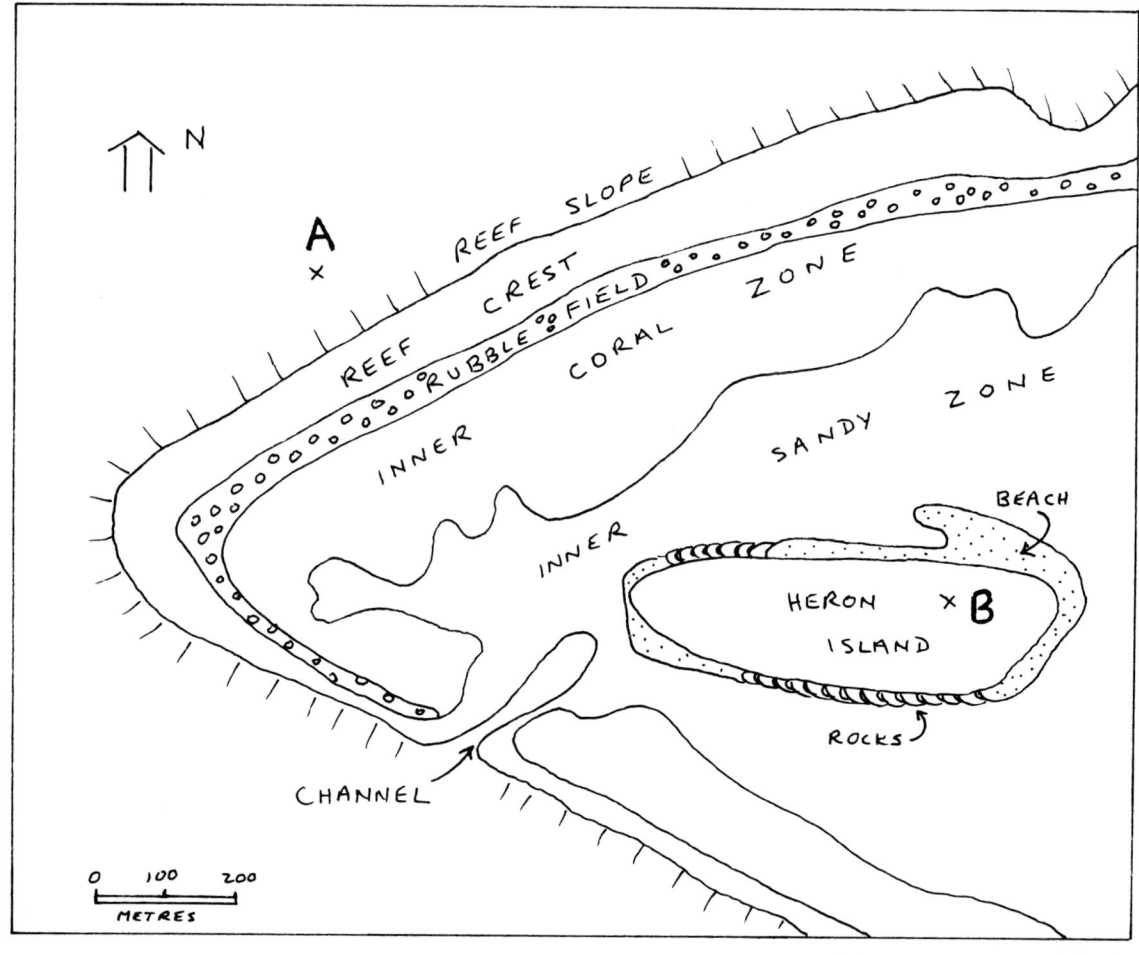

damage by keeping to the sandy pathways as much as possible and avoid walking on the fragile corals," he recommends. "If you turn a rock over, be sure to put it back or the animals which live there may die."

You enter the water opposite the dive shop. At first you are walking on white coral sand, with just a few widely spaced patches of coral. Green algae grow over much of the coral and bright green turtle weed provides shelter for some small crabs.

Cary picks up a brilliant blue starfish, about 15cm across and with a rough surface. "This starfish is called a linkia," he announces. "When you turn it over you can see the mouth in the middle and a broad groove down each arm. Hundreds of little suction pads are used for walking and clinging on to objects."

Can you draw a cross section of the coral platform from A to B, labelling the following?
(a) beach
(b) inner sandy zone
(c) inner coral zone
(d) rubble field
(e) reef crest
(f) reef slope
(g) low tide level

◀ 43 *Sections of the coral platform around Heron Island.*

44 *Reef walkers.*

The inner coral zone

This is where you find sea cucumbers (*Holothuria* or *bêche-de-mer*). They look like big brown cucumbers, but are, in fact, animals related to the starfish. In some Asian countries they are eaten as a delicacy.

Sea cucumbers use bushy tentacles to feed sand and organic material into their mouths. Their rudimentary alimentary canal then sifts out anything of nutritional value and this is digested.

This zone is a sheltered part of the reef where parrot fish and tusk fish come to feed. And, if you are lucky, you will glimpse a blue-spotted stingray before it glides away.

You can get a clear view of the marine life beneath the surface by using a tray or bucket with a transparent plastic or glass bottom to it.

Cary points out a small and harmless brown epaulette shark. On another day you might see a small shovel-nose shark. Both are more interested in catching tiny crabs than in attacking a person.

The reef crest

At the far edge of the reef platform is a crest or

ridge. The crest completely encircles the whole of Heron Reef. It presents a strong barrier to the pounding waves. In high seas boulders of coral have been flung over the outer edge of the reef, creating a boulder zone or rubble field. The boulders provide shelter for starfish, crabs and various molluscs. The dead coral will eventually be broken right down and will be added to the sand on the beach.

The reef crest protects the large, leathery green or brown, soft coral called sarcophyton, which grows on the leeward side of the barrier. Close examination reveals this coral to consist of hundreds of tiny white polyp tentacles which trap and paralyse plankton and tiny floating animals such as shrimps. Only a few of the daisy-like polyps come out to feed during the day; most hide in their tubular skeletons until dark.

Coral's predators

Polyps contain waxes and fats which provide food for certain varieties of fish. Although the limestone skeleton of hard coral protects it from most predators, the parrot fish is not deterred, and crunches his way through the skeleton to reach the soft polyp. The crown of thorns starfish also eats coral and can destroy large areas of the reef.

Not all coral is reef-building coral. Soft corals do not have rigid limestone skeletons. Each soft coral waving in the current is a colony of identical polyps connected by fleshy tissue.

You would think that soft corals would be totally defenceless and be snapped up by all sorts of fish. Yet very few marine animals eat soft corals. Some soft corals contain chemicals which are toxic to fish; others have small needles of limestone, called spicules, protecting the polyps.

If you stand on the outer edge of the reef crest you can look down into deep, clear water where the branching staghorn corals flourish in forests of limestone. The best way to see the coral without even getting wet is to take the Yellow Sub.

A Yellow Submarine

There's a buzz of excitement as everyone files down into the hull of Subsea Explorer II, nicknamed the Yellow Sub. The sides of the hull are windows, looking straight out onto the reef.

You sit in pairs with your head just below sea level. Soothing music plays as you motor out of the small, man-made harbour. Then, as you reach the reef wall, the guide talks about what

45 Inside the Yellow Submarine. ▶

can be seen through the windows.

"Staghorn is our fastest-growing coral, up to 25cm a year," she says as you glide past a jungle of light-brown coral. "And there's a turtle on the port side." A thick-necked loggerhead swims effortlessly by, with a gentle beat of its flippers.

Next she points out a spotted eagle ray rippling by, and a small white-tip reef shark.

Mingling within the corals are fish with names as exotic as their appearance: butterfly fish, speckled sweetlips, zebra fish, coral trout, trumpet fish, sergeant majors, even a humbug fish with black and white stripes. It is as if a paintbrush has gone out of control, with bright blotches of colour, stripes and spots.

An hour is too short a time to spend in this coral wonderland. For a closer look you will have to take to water yourself...

9
Taking the plunge

Snorkelling

"If you have never been snorkelling before," says Janine to a small group of people by the pool, "today's experience is going to change your life! You're going to see things that will leave you spellbound."

She shows you how to put on a mask, then

explains: "A mask keeps the water away from your eyes and this enables you to see clearly underwater. Without it everything would appear blurred. When you use a snorkel you don't have to keep lifting your head up to take a breath of air. And fins help you move easily, without using all your energy thrashing about trying to stay up."

This means that you can float on the surface, face down, with a ring-side view of the activities of the marine community.

46 A snorkel lesson.

After a snorkel lesson in the pool, Janine takes you to the reef flat where small islands of coral emerge from the sand.

Putting on the mask and snorkel, you kneel down in just one metre of water and put your face on the surface. You can hardly believe how clear it is. A few tiny fish dart off to shelter behind a rock. The reds, greens and yellows of the coral and the turtle grass shine brightly in the dappled sunlight.

It all looks larger than life. And, in fact, it is.... Water makes objects look larger and nearer than they really are. You can illustrate this by holding a pencil upright in a glass of water.

The part of the pencil below the surface will look thicker than the rest. This happens because light is refracted, or "bent", when it passes from water to air. Hold the pencil at an

47 Pencils in a glass of water.

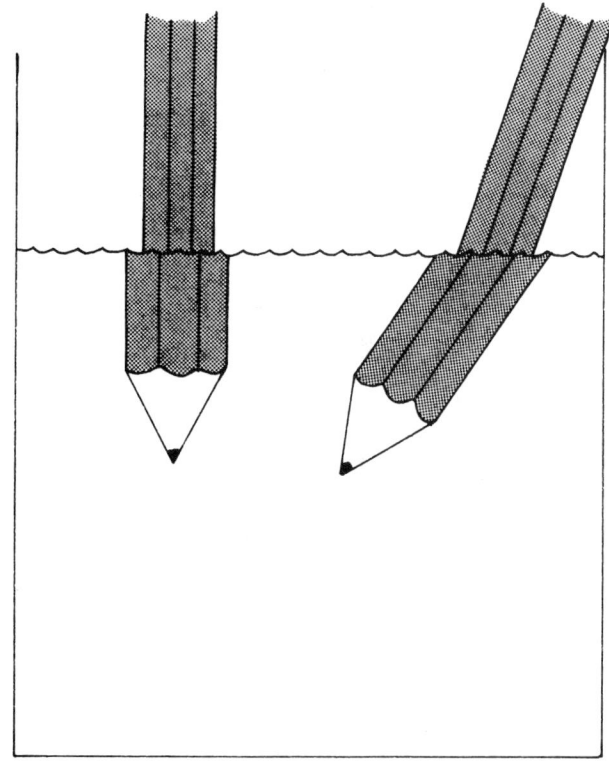

49

angle and it appears to bend because the light has been refracted.

If you are wearing a mask and looking, with your eyes at surface level, at someone waist-deep in a swimming pool, the bottom half of his or her body appears to be too large for the top half.

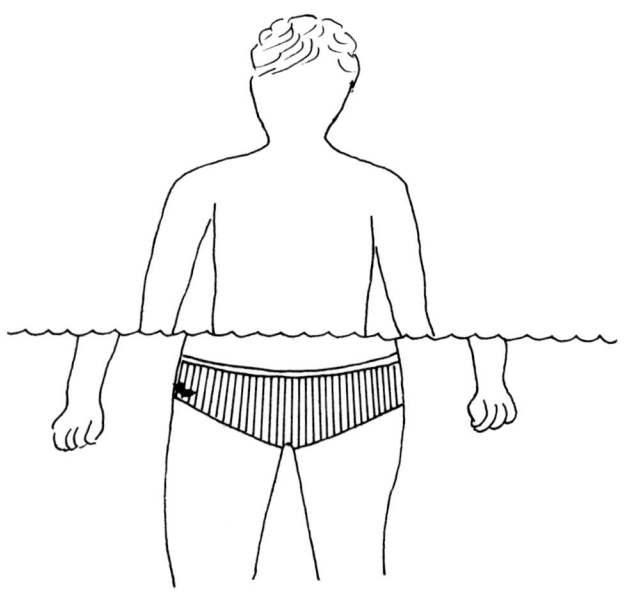

48 Looking at someone waist-deep in water.

49 Objects underwater seem bigger and closer than they really are.

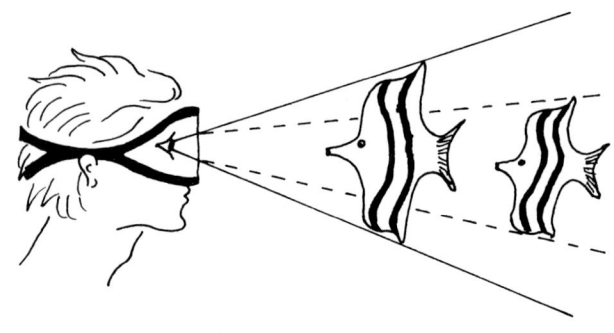

In the same way, fish and coral seen underwater look a third bigger than they really are.

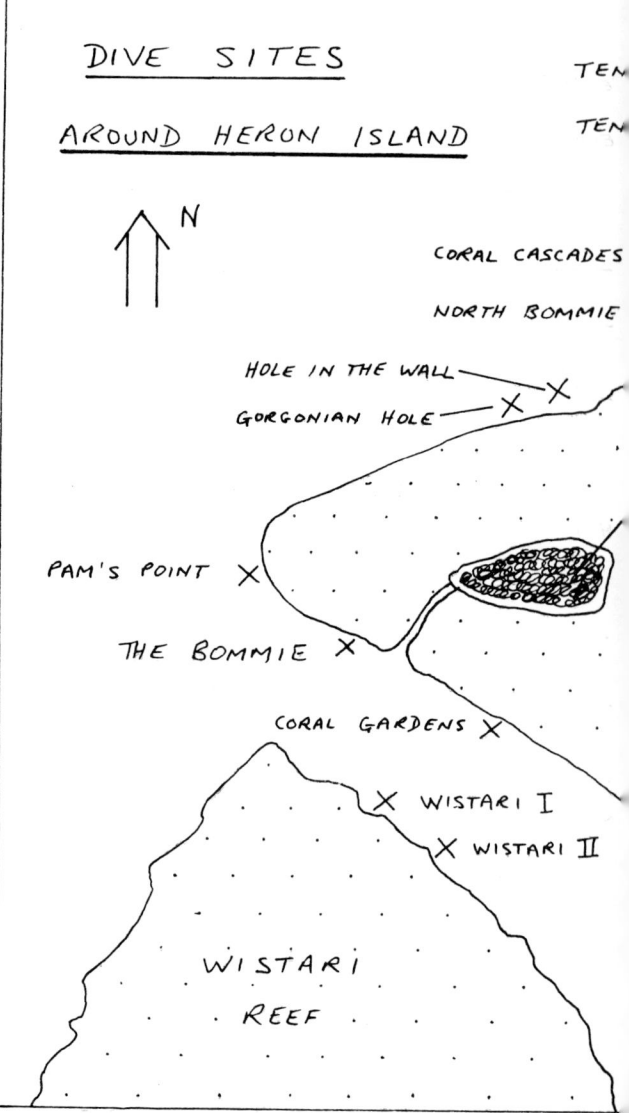

Scuba diving

If snorkelling is a window looking onto the reef, then scuba diving is the door which lets you in. With a cylinder of compressed air on your back you have a passport into a realm which is hidden from most people. But the passport is valid for only as long as your air lasts — normally 40-60 minutes.

Ever since Jacques Cousteau and his colleague Emile Gagnan developed the Self-Contained Underwater Breathing Apparatus (SCUBA) more and more people have been

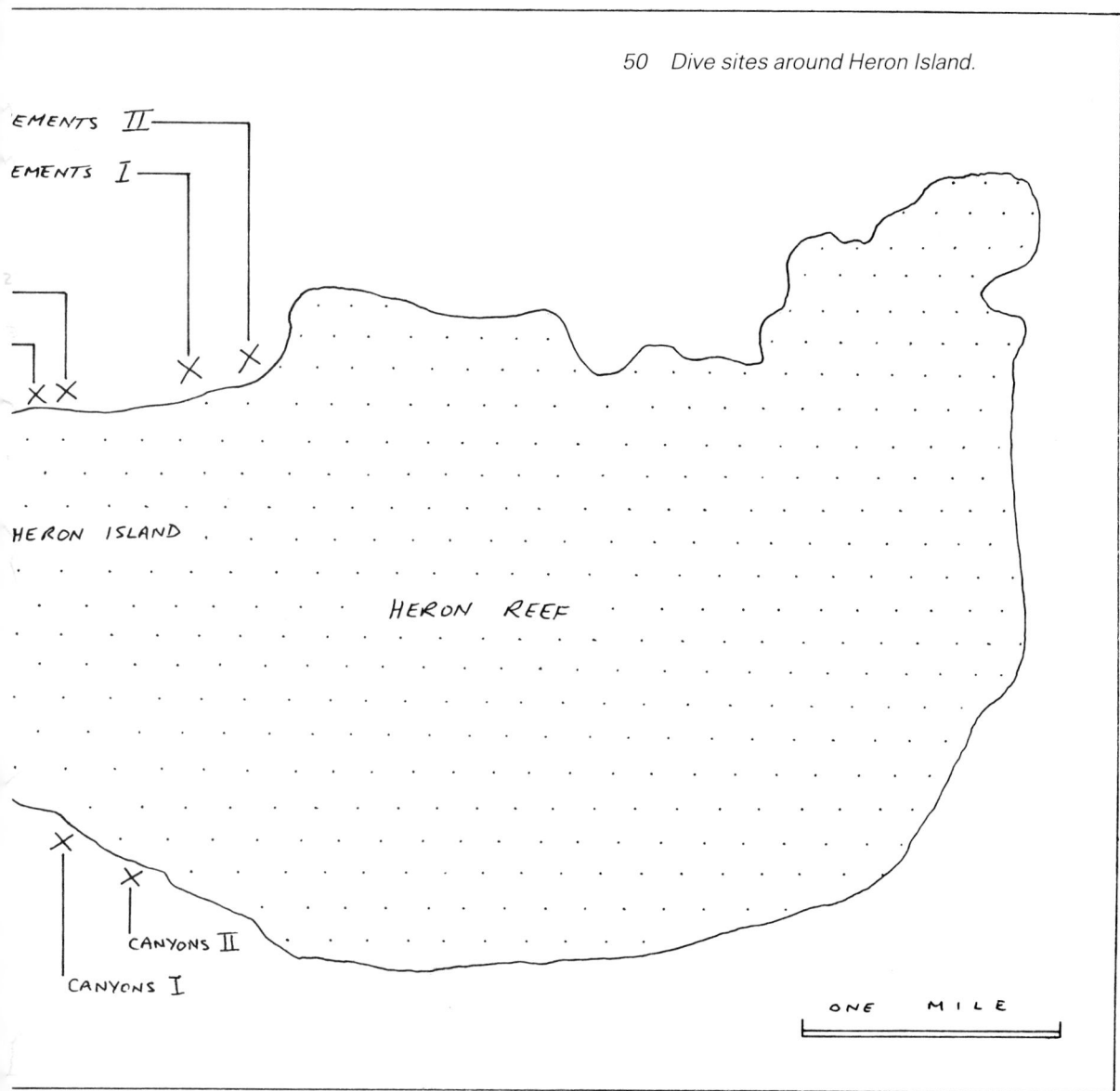

50 Dive sites around Heron Island.

able to experience the underwater world at first hand.

Normally, only qualified scuba divers can use the dive equipment on Heron Island, but the dive centre does also run courses of instruction for novices.

Before going diving you should be a competent swimmer and moderately fit. The human body was not designed to exist underwater, so you need specialized equipment and proper training. With the emphasis on safety you always wear a lifejacket, dive in pairs and keep an eye on your "buddy". You must learn the principles of diving or else you risk getting the "bends", a burst eardrum or burst lung.

Diving around Heron Island

All dive sites are within twenty minutes of the resort; some are much nearer. Pam's Point is named after one of Chris Poulson's daughters.

You make your way down to the harbour, carrying mask, snorkel and fins, and wearing a thin wet suit as protection against coral

51 Loading the dive boat.

52 On the way to the dive site. ▶

scratches. The heavy air cylinders are brought down on a trailer.

Everyone lends a hand by forming a human chain to load the boat with all the gear.

Last-minute preparations are made as the boat motors out to the dive site. Then, when you and your buddy are ready, the dive master gives the "OK" signal and you roll backwards off the side of the boat into the water.

As you plunge beneath the surface, the cries of the seagulls and voices of people on the boat are silenced. All you can hear is a hissing noise as you suck in air, and the bass gurgle of your exhaled bubbles.

Exchanging the "OK" signal with your buddy, you float gently down, enjoying the sensation of drifting weightlessly through forests of stone.

Visibility varies between 10m and 25m. The water temperature is around 17°C (62°F) in July and August, and 23°C (73°F) in January and February.

Dives from Heron Island do not exceed 20m, so there is little danger of the "bends", associated with deeper dives.

Enchanting kingdom

You are now over the reef wall, well beyond the probing eyes of the reef walkers. As the underwater world opens out you swim past staghorn and brain coral, sea cucumbers, nudibranchs, anemones, starfish, clams, coral-eating fish, then the fish that eat the coral-eaters.

A harmless manta ray, 4m across, glides serenely through this blue-rinsed landscape. A curious reef shark circles to take a look at the latest batch of intruders into his kingdom.

But aren't they dangerous? Sharks, barracuda and other aquatic nasties? It *is* true that it can be pretty lively down here, especially at night when the hunters emerge to search for their evening meal. But the fish in these waters are too well-fed to bother tackling something as difficult as a person.

Columns of coral stretch up from the sea bed

53 A diver feeding the fish off Heron Island.

to just below the surface. These giant coral heads are called Bommies or Bomboras, and provide sanctuary for countless marine creatures.

Underwater film-maker Valerie Taylor has described Heron's fish life as "the richest and most diverse collection of tame tropical fish found anywhere in the world".

Some estimates say the Great Barrier Reef has 1,500 species of fish and 400 species of coral. Some are found nowhere else in the world.

Seeing the arrival of divers is like hearing the dinner gong for the tamer species around the island. They swim up and nudge you, asking for some of the bread and meat you are holding in a plastic bag. A 1.6m grouper, or potato cod, graciously accepts a morsel from you. Even the moray eels join in, though you must be on your best behaviour because they can clamp their teeth onto your finger and refuse to let go if you don't treat them with respect.

It is far from being a silent world; you can hear parrot fish crunching the coral, someone's cylinder knock against a rock, and the distant noise of a motor boat. Sound is transmitted much faster in water than in air, although you cannot tell which direction it comes from.

As you fin slowly along, you enjoy the sensation of gliding like a bird through underwater forests and coral gardens teeming with colourful tenants.

But all too soon your air contents gauge indicates that it is time to return to the boat. Two hours after leaving the shore you are back on the island. This is the first time you have seen such a beautiful kaleidoscope of life and colour, and it is the most exhilarating two hours you have ever spent.

10
Interests of science

The research station

Next to the resort on Heron Island is a research station which is run by the University of Queensland. It was established by the Great Barrier Reef Committee in 1951. Since the first building was completed in 1952, the station has provided a base for both research and education on anything associated with this coral island.

Dr Ian Lawn is the director, with overall responsibility for the administration of the centre and the programme of research which is carried out there.

"Very few research stations in the world are actually on a coral cay," says Dr Lawn. "And this is the only one on top of a large coral platform. This gives us quick and easy access by foot or boat to the study sites."

Other islands off the Queensland coast have field or research stations — One Tree Island, Orpheus Island and Lizard Island — but the one on Heron Island is the largest and most active. It is perhaps the world's greatest marine laboratory, with computers, high-powered microscopes, live specimen tanks fed by water straight from the sea, a museum and library. There are also boating and diving facilities and a photographic darkroom. Diving and

54 *The board depicts some of the subjects of study.*

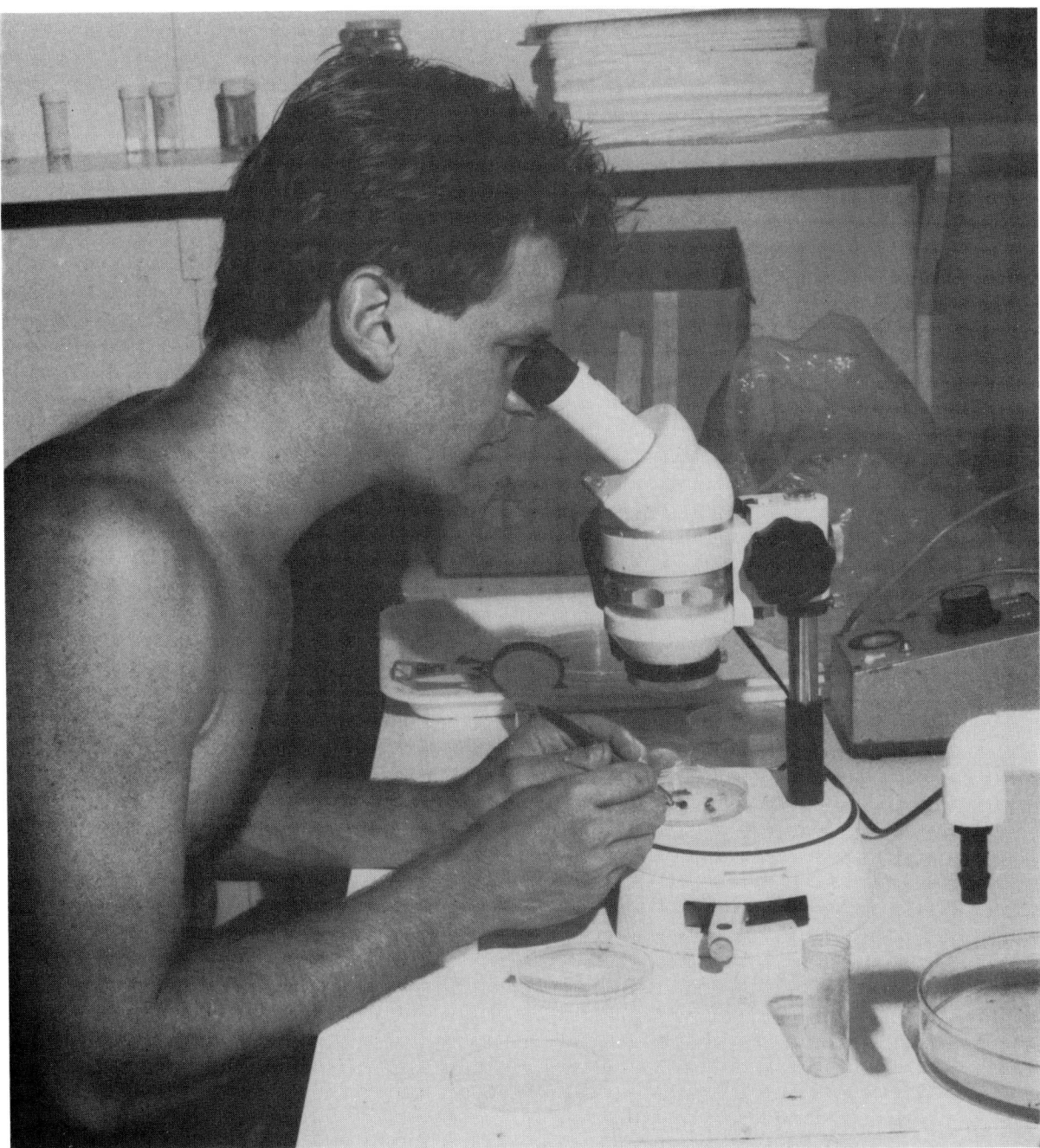

55 *Taking a close look at marine life.*

photography play an important role here. Why should they be more important on Heron Island than on a mainland research station?

The success of the station has been made possible by funding from a number of sources, especially the University of Queensland.

Nine permanent staff include the director, secretary, scientific research officer, laboratory attendant, boat and diving officer, maintenance officer, maintenance assistant, groundsman and cleaner.

Research students

Students from throughout Australia as well as from abroad, especially the USA and the UK, visit the station to carry out research or take part in educational courses. The station can accommodate up to eighty visitors, and over one thousand people use it each year — about ten per cent of whom come from abroad. Unlike the guests of the holiday resort, those who come to the research station make their own beds and cook their own meals.

"We're here to provide facilities for independent investigations," says Dr Lawn. "At any one time a variety of studies will be in progress. One person or group will be trying to understand how marine animals control their behaviour. For example, one species may have an apparently simple nervous system, yet display a very complicated pattern of behaviour. We hope research will tell us why.

"Other research looks at how quickly different corals grow again after being damaged. The relatively fast-growing staghorn coral is not unduly affected by damage caused by people or storms. But brain coral, for example, grows very slowly, so its existence is more readily threatened."

The crown of thorns starfish eats coral. Recent waves of these destructive starfish have left vast tracks of the reef devoid of life. This has given rise to considerable concern, especially in the northern half of the Great Barrier Reef where some tourist resorts are losing their coral. More research into the reasons for, and long-term effects of, the starfish attacks will help produce an appropriate strategy to deal with the problem.

56 Rules for conservation. Can you think of any others?

The station has set up various fauna reserves on Heron Island, out of bounds to tourists. They are areas maintained solely for the conservation of the natural habitat, to protect species and permit scientific research.

Other programmes include recording rainfall and atmospheric pressure; monitoring water samples for nutrients, salinity and temperature; and collecting data on the size and numbers of local populations of coral trout.

Park rangers

In November 1982 the Queensland National Parks and Wildlife Service set up a ranger station on Heron Island. "We patrol the reefs and islands of the area to check that everything is OK," says one of the rangers. "Everything is zoned for particular uses, so we have to make sure that people aren't fishing in a restricted area or spearfishing using scuba gear."

There are a couple of rangers here at any one time and they live on Heron Island for fifteen days each month. "We are really here as a 'presence' to encourage people to be conservation-minded. We check campers' permits, pick up litter and maybe take people on a reef walk."

Conflict and cooperation

Representatives from the University of Queensland, Heron Island Pty Ltd and Queensland National Parks and Wildlife Service jointly make up an island council. The function of this group is to develop a comprehensive management plan for the island, and iron out some of the conflicts that have occurred in the past.

Can you suggest what conflicts of interest could have existed among the resort managers, the research station and the rangers?

The council contributes to the well-being of Heron Island by, for example, organizing revegetation and landscaping. When experts are brought in to improve the harbour or work on new buildings, the resort houses them and provides transport. The research station brings in people to solve ecological problems — such as how the fish life is affected by the dumping of discarded meat in the water. And the National Parks and Wildlife Service decides such things as where to put particular plants in order to give a canopy to screen the less sightly buildings.

In their different ways they are all working for the good of the island and the Great Barrier Reef as a whole. Using just one sentence for each, describe what benefit can be gained from: (a) bringing tourists to the island
(b) researching turtle behaviour
(c) patrolling the reefs and islands.

PS... Blueprint for survival

Heron Island offers us a glimpse into a very special world. This is an island which emerged from the ocean on the backs of billions of coral polyps. It has witnessed a reversal of approaches, from the wholesale slaughter of turtles to the caring nature of conservationists. It has seen the planned development of a holiday resort and the establishment of a research station and ranger station. Thousands of sea birds flock around the island daily, turtles still come to lay their eggs on the beach, and fish populations of the surrounding reefs are on the increase.

Heron Island is an open zoo, with no walls or cages. As a visitor you become a part of the living community. In the past, the isolation of the Great Barrier Reef has helped ensure its survival. But now the Reef is becoming more and more accessible and the pressures on it are growing.

The Great Barrier Reef Marine Park Authority is working towards a comprehensive approach to conservation and public use and enjoyment of the entire Reef area. They are aiming for a compromise which is best for everyone in the long term. It is a question of balancing the need to conserve the Reef and its prolific plant and animal life, with human needs – commercial and amateur fishing, scuba diving, boating, shell collecting, reef-based tourist facilities, education and scientific research.

Without certain controls much of our own environment could be ruined. For example, someone might start dumping rubbish in the middle of the residential area where we live. Or large areas of attractive woodland may be cut down unnecessarily to make way for building which could be located elsewhere. Unused derelict sites may be left undeveloped while people remain homeless.

There is often a conflict of interests between those who want to develop land for economic gains and those who are more concerned with the quality of life.

What are some of the societies and associations which are working towards making our environment a better place to live? Where is the nearest national park to your home? Why was that particular area chosen?

Threats

Despite the Marine Park's efforts, the presence of humans is still a constant threat to plant and animal life on and near the Reef:

- Certain commercial interests want to explore the Great Barrier Reef for oil. Others want to mine the reefs for limestone.
- Ships carrying oil and other toxic cargoes risk spillage or more major disasters.
- Over-fishing of giant clams and other marine life by foreign fishermen is not adequately controlled.
- More and more people are using the Reef, yet we know little about the long-term impact of such pressure.
- Commercial shell, coral and aquarium fish collecting goes on in many parts of the Reef.
- Polluted water, including silt and pesticides, from Queensland's coastal waterways is being carried over the Reef.

People today have great control over their environment. Therefore it is largely in our hands to decide how well Heron Island and the Great Barrier Reef as a whole will survive. Exploitation or conservation? Somewhere between the two there is a balance.

Heron Island is very small; its resources are finite and its flora and fauna can be easily damaged. Although our country is much larger than Heron Island it still suffers when it is not looked after.

What would happen to our trees if there were no replanting programme? Why is it illegal to pick wild cowslips or take eggs from an osprey's nest? What is your attitude towards litter? And how do you view the different types of pollution? And what about nuclear waste?

Perhaps the lessons learned on Heron Island can teach us something about how we should treat the area where we live.

Perhaps Heron should be a blueprint for our attitudes towards our own environment and the world as a whole.

Glossary

alimentary canal passage through which food passes into the body
altitude height above sea level
aquatic growing or living in or near water
biodegradable decomposes naturally
botanist someone who studies botany, the science of plants
cay coral island
combustible capable of burning
conservation preservation
consolidate solidify; combine into one whole
crustacean aquatic animal with a hard shell, such as a crab or lobster
cyclone tropical storm with strong winds caused by a depression or low-pressure system
data facts
decompose break down or rot
dehydrated deprived of water
desalination removal of salt
ecology study of animal and plant behaviour in relation to their surroundings
environment surroundings; region; landscape
fauna animal life
finite limited; not infinite
fledgling young bird
flora plant life
flying buttress support which helps to hold up a building or tree
generator apparatus for producing power — electricity, gas, steam, etc
guano sea bird droppings
habitat natural home of plant or animal
hatchling animal which has recently hatched
herbivorous eats only plants
incinerator a container used to burn material, reducing it to ashes
incubate hatch eggs by keeping them warm

kaleidoscope constantly changing collection of bright colours
lease contract to occupy land for a specified time
leeward the side or direction which is sheltered from the wind
migratory moving from one place to another, usually with the seasons
mollusc soft-bodied animal, usually with a hard shell, such as cuttle fish, oyster or mussel
mucus slimy substance secreted by some animals
nutrients food providing nourishment
omnivorous eats anything
palatable tasty
perishable liable to perish; subject to rapid decay
plankton tiny plant and animal particles floating in sea water, usually invisible to the naked eye
pollution harmful impurities in the environment
precarious uncertain; dependent on chance
predator animal that preys on others
prolific abundant
resources materials needed for an activity
rudimentary basic
salinity the degree of saltiness of the water
spectrum rays of light split into a series of colours
strategy plan of campaign
subsidiary supplementary; secondary
symbiosis relationship between two living organisms, in which both benefit
toxic poisonous
Tropic of Cancer parallel of latitude 23° 26'30"N
Tropic of Capricorn parallel of latitude 23° 26'30"S
vulnerable without defences, susceptible to injury
zoologist someone who studies animals

Further reading

Australia, a travel survival kit, by Tony Wheeler, Lonely Planet, 1983 (third edition)
The Australian Great Barrier Reef in colour, by Keith Gillett, Reed, 1968
Australia's underwater wilderness, editor Roland Hughes, Weldon, 1985
Australia: this land these people, Reader's Digest, 1971
The complete scuba diving guide, by Dave Saunders, A & C Black, 1987
Corals of the Great Barrier Reef, by Walt Deas & S. Domm, Ure Smith, 1976
Discover Australia, by Robert Wilson, Merehurst, 1986
A field guide to the reef fishes of tropical Australia and the Indo-Pacific region, by R.H. Carcasson, Collins, 1977
Great Barrier Reef, by Allan Power, Paul Hamlyn, 1969
The Great Barrier Reef, by Isobel Bennett, Merehurst, 1981 (fourth impression)
The Great Barrier Reef: a divers' guide, editor P. Saenger, Australian Underwater Federation, 1977
Great Barrier Reef of Australia, its products and potentialities, by W. Saville-Kent, John Curry O'Neill, 1972
Insight guides, Australia, APA Productions, Harrap, 1985
Islands of Australia, by D. Baglin & B. Mullins, Ure Smith, 1974
Narrative of a surveying voyage of HMS Fly, by Joseph Beete Jukes, T & W Boone, 1847
Reader's Digest Book of the Great Barrier Reef, 1984
Sea turtles, by Robert Bustard, Collins, 1972
The struggle for the Great Barrier Reef, by Patricia Clare, Collins, 1971

Other books by Dave Saunders:

Through the year in the Caribbean, Batsford, 1981
The West Indians in Britain, Batsford, 1984
The complete scuba diving guide, A & C Black, 1987

Index

algae, 12
Anchor Island, 6
Auckland, 30
Ayers Rock, 30

birds, 5, 9, 13, 18, 19, 28, 30, 31, 33, 34, 35, 40
Bommie, Bombora, 55
Brisbane, 10, 17, 22, 28, 30, 41

Capricorn Group, 7, 13, 17, 37, 41
Capricornia Section, 7, 8
cay, 10, 13, 14, 15, 35, 56
clams, 12
climate, 8, 9
colour absorption, 11
conservation, 18, 19, 30, 31, 59, 60, 61
continental shelf, 10
convolvuli, 13, 36
Cook, Captain James, 6
coral, 6, 9, 10, 11, 12, 13, 14, 15, 17, 18, 19, 20, 26, 28, 44, 45, 46, 47, 50, 51, 53, 55, 56, 58, 60
Cousteau, Jacques, 50
crabs, 40, 46
creepers, 13
crown of thorns starfish, 46, 58
cyclone, 9

desalination, 22
dive centre, diving, 27, 28, 29, 50, 51, 52, 55, 56, 60

electricity, 18, 19, 20

fishing, 8, 17, 18, 19, 30, 33, 59, 60

Gladstone, 8, 10, 17, 22, 24
Great Barrier Reef, 6, 7, 8, 9, 10, 11, 12, 15, 30, 43, 56, 59, 60, 61
Great Barrier Reef Marine Park Authority, 60
guano, 13, 33

gulls, 34, 35

harbour, 17, 28, 46, 51
helicopter, 24, 25, 26
Heron Island Pty Ltd, 18, 59
Heron Reef, 8, 14, 26, 28
herons, 9, 15, 34, 35

interpretive centre, 27, 28

Jukes, Joseph Beete, 15

Lady Elliott Island, 6, 7, 11
latitude, 6, 7, 11
lifejacket, 24, 51
Lizard Island, 56
London, 8, 9, 30
longitude, 6, 7

marine park, 7, 8
monsoon, 9
mutton bird, shearwater, 33, 34, 35

national park, 18, 60
National Parks & Wildlife Service, 27, 43, 59
New York, 8, 9
noddy tern, 9, 31, 32, 33, 34

oil, 18, 60
One Tree Island, 56
Opera House, 30
Orpheus Island, 56

Pacific Ocean, 6, 9
pandanus tree, 34, 35, 36
Papua New Guinea, 6, 41
Peninsula & Orient (P & O) Ltd, 18
pisonia tree, 13, 15, 31, 32, 33, 35
plankton, 10, 12, 46
plants, 5, 12, 13, 18, 31, 35, 60
polyps, 10, 11, 12, 46, 60
Poulson, Chris, 17, 18, 21, 51

Queensland, 6, 7, 10, 16, 17, 24, 30, 41, 43, 56, 57, 59, 60

rail, banded land-rail, 35
rainfall, 8, 9
rangers, ranger station, 19, 20, 37, 38, 59, 60
reef, 6, 9, 10, 11, 13, 14, 17, 19, 26, 28, 29, 37, 40, 41, 44, 45, 46, 49, 53, 59, 60
reef heron, 9, 15, 34, 35
research station, 19, 20, 27, 56-59, 60
resort, 14, 18, 19, 20, 26, 27, 30, 31, 32, 40, 44, 58, 59, 60
rubbish, 18, 20, 60

San Francisco, 30
sea cucumbers, 12, 45
sea urchins, 12
shearwater, mutton bird, 33, 34
shells, 18
she-oak, casuarina, 13, 35
Siberia, 34
snorkel, snorkelling, 28, 29, 48, 49, 50, 51
Solomon Islands, 41
starfish, 12, 45, 46, 53, 58
Sydney, 8
symbiosis, 12

temperature, 8, 9, 40, 52, 59
Tokyo, 30
tourists, 17
Tropic of Cancer, 7
Tropic of Capricorn, 7, 8, 10, 41
turtles, 9, 16, 17, 18, 19, 28, 30, 35, 36, 37-43, 47, 59, 60

University of Queensland, 56, 57, 59

Whitsunday Islands, 13
Wilson Island, 15
Wistari Reef, 8, 14

Yellow Submarine, 28, 29, 46